Basic internet skills

Other Books of Interest

* * * * *

Acknowledgements

The author and publishers would like to thank Oxford Cambridge and RSA Examinations for permission to refer to their Internet Technologies Stage 1 course on which the exercises and self-assessment checklists in this book have been based. We would also like to thank AOL UK for their help with Chapter 6.

Basic Internet skills

Jim Gatenby

BERNARD BABANI (publishing) LTD
The Grampians
Shepherds Bush Road
London W6 7NF
England

www.babanibooks.com

Please Note

Although every care has been taken with the production of this book to ensure that any projects, designs, modifications and/or programs, etc., contained herewith, operate in a correct and safe manner and also that any components specified are normally available in Great Britain, the Publishers and Author do not accept responsibility in any way for the failure (including fault in design) of any project, design, modification or program to work correctly or to cause damage to any equipment that it may be connected to or used in conjunction with, or in respect of any other damage or injury that may be so caused, nor do the Publishers accept responsibility in any way for the failure to obtain specified components.

Notice is also given that if equipment that is still under warranty is modified in any way or used or connected with home-built equipment then that warranty may be void.

© 2001 BERNARD BABANI (publishing) LTD

First Published - September 2001

British Library Cataloguing in Publication Data:

A catalogue record for this book is available from the
British Library

ISBN 0 85934 494 0
Cover Design by Gregor Arthur
Printed and bound in Great Britain by The Guernsey Press

About this Book

Many of us start using the Internet in a haphazard, hit and miss fashion. Initially we just log on and start surfing the Net, hoping to find something interesting. This book aims to provide a more structured approach to using the Internet and the powerful tools it provides.

The first chapter covers electronic mail, including sending, receiving, forwarding and replying to e-mails. Useful features such as file attachments and address books are described. The chapter also covers choosing an Internet Service Provider and connecting to the Internet.

Retrieving information is covered in the second chapter. The various types of search tools - search engines, directories and search agents - are described, together with basic techniques for making searches more focused and successful. Methods of saving and printing text and graphics extracted from Web pages are also discussed.

The remainder of the book describes the creation of your own Web pages. First, writing your own code in the HTML language is covered. At least a smattering of knowledge of this subject is considered essential even if you eventually create your pages using Web design software. This latter topic is discussed in Chapter 5. The final chapter describes the publishing of Web pages, including uploading to the Internet and attracting visitors to your site.

The text should be useful both to the general reader and to students of introductory Internet courses such as Becoming WebWise from the BBC and the Internet Technologies Stage 1 course from Oxford Cambridge and RSA Examinations. Relevant practice exercises and skills checklists are included throughout the text. Details of the syllabus for Internet Technologies Stage 1 are given in the Appendix, together with a list of relevant publications from Oxford Cambridge and RSA Examinations. These include sample practical assignments.

About the Author

Jim Gatenby trained as a Chartered Mechanical Engineer and initially worked at Rolls-Royce Ltd using computers in the analysis of performance. He obtained a Master of Philosophy degree in Mathematical Education by research and taught mathematics and computing for many years. His most recent posts have included Head of Computer Studies and Information Technology Coordinator. During this time he has written many books in the fields of educational computing and Microsoft Windows.

For several years the author successfully taught the well-established CLAIT course (Computer Literacy and Information Technology) from Oxford Cambridge and RSA Examinations, as well as GCSE and National Curriculum Information Technology courses.

Trademarks

Contents

4

Creating Web Pages by Writing HTML Code   69

5

Creating Web Pages Using an HTML Editor   101

6

Publishing Your Web Site   131

Appendix: The Internet Technologies Stage 1 Course   149

Index   151

Electronic Mail

Introduction

E-mail is one of the most heavily used facilities on the Internet. It has revolutionized communication between people and altered forever the everyday routines in the office and work place. E-mail is an alternative to the conventional letter post, the fax, the telephone call and the personal visit. On the negative side, the sheer convenience of e-mail means some people are overwhelmed trying to reply to several dozen e-mails a day. Many of these are unsolicited junk mail, known as "spam". Some people miss the human contact allowed by more traditional methods of communication, such as face-to-face conversations. Previous more leisurely times allowed people to indulge in the art of letter writing; e-mail aficionados favour a cut-down version of English in which style has been replaced by brevity in the form of abbreviations and acronyms, such as "TNX" for "thanks".

The E-mail Process

Internet Explorer includes its own e-mail program, Outlook Express. Such a program, known as an *e-mail client*, allows you to type in new e-mails and to read and store the e-mails sent to you by other people.

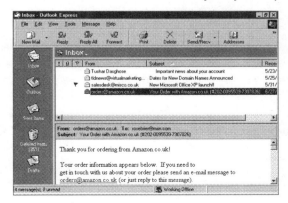

You would normally create a new e-mail message working *off-line*, after clicking **New Mail**, as shown below on the left.

When you've entered your message, along with the e-mail address of the intended recipient, you would give the command to send the e-mail. Initially the message will be placed in the **Outbox**, shown on the left. As soon as you connect to the Internet, the message is sent to the mail server of your Internet Service Provider, such as MSN or AOL. A copy of your outgoing message will be kept in the **Sent Items** box on your computer, shown below on the left. The computer handling the outgoing mail at your ISP is known as an **SMTP Server** (Simple Mail Transfer Protocol). Then the message is delivered and stored at the mail server of the recipient's Internet Service Provider. The computer handling the incoming mail at the ISP is known as a POP3 (Post Office Protocol) server. Next time the recipient reads their e-mail, the new messages are downloaded to the **Inbox** on their computer and saved on their hard disc.

So when you send someone an e-mail, the message is not directly transmitted to their computer. Although the e-mail may arrive at the recipient's ISP mail server in a matter of seconds, it will sit there unread until the recipient checks their mailbox. Of course, if you arrange to send important mail to a friend or colleague who is standing by to receive it, the whole process can be completed in a few seconds. Used in this way e-mail is much faster then conventional methods.

A major feature of e-mail is the sending of *attachments*. These are files of any sort - text, graphics, spreadsheet, sound, etc., which are "clipped" to an e-mail message and sent along with it. I have used this method to send complete books to the printers. Although very large files can take an hour or two to transmit electronically between computers, via the telephone lines, manuscripts sent by conventional post can take days.

E-mail also avoids the expense and inconvenience of packing and posting. Distance is irrelevant - the cost is just the charge for a local telephone call.

Another major advantage of e-mail over conventional mail, is the ease with which you can send multiple copies to a wide circulation list, without the need to physically address lots of envelopes, etc. You simply select the recipients' names from your electronic address book, which is created by the e-mail program. If you're involved in sensitive work, you can send "blind copies" so that recipients don't know who else has received a copy.

There are e-mail features to automate the sending of an immediate reply to a message and to forward a copy of a message to someone else. You can arrange to be automatically notified when someone has read an e-mail that you have sent to them.

E-mails remove much of the clutter of the conventional letter post on paper, although a hard copy can be printed if necessary. E-mails can be organised efficiently into folders.

Whereas a copy of a document, graphic, or photograph, etc., transmitted by a fax system may be of dubious quality, files sent as e-mail attachments should be as good as the original.

E-mail programs like Outlook Express and Eudora Pro allow the text of the message to be formatted with different fonts, graphics and in the HTML code used in Web pages, including links to Web sites.

Many Web sites now include links designed to encourage visitors to contact them via e-mail. Obviously this feature is heavily exploited by businesses seeking orders, but it's equally useful for any organization or individual wanting to gather information or start a debate. For example, someone researching their family tree may solicit responses from other family members visiting the site. When a visitor clicks a link of the type **Send us an e-mail**, their own e-mail program opens up with the reply address automatically inserted. The visitor only needs to type in the text of their message and click **Send**.

E-mail Requirements

The Windows CD provides all of the software tools needed to set up your machine to start sending and receiving e-mails. There is also alternative software from companies other than Microsoft, such as Eudora Pro from Qualcomm Incorporated.

Since e-mail is an integral part of the Internet, getting connected to the Net is the first priority. At one time this was quite complex but now with later versions of Windows and its Internet Connection Wizard the task is quite easy.

A PC capable of running Windows is the basic requirement, with a modem correctly set up and connected to a telephone line. In order to send and receive electronic mail, you also need:

* A Connection to the Internet provided by an Internet Service Provider (ISP) or an Online Service.

* An E-mail Program such as Outlook Express or Eudora Pro.

* An E-mail Address

Connections to the Internet

In order to use the Internet (for both e-mail and browsing the World Wide Web), you need to open an *account* with a company providing Internet access.

Before starting the process to connect to the Internet, you must first choose an Internet Service Provider (ISP). This is a company with fast and powerful computers (known as *servers*) directly connected to the Internet. The ordinary user connects to the Internet via the ISP servers, in most cases using a modem and telephone line. Part of the setup process includes the creation of a *dial-up connection* to enable your modem to dial the telephone number of the ISP's server computer.

This will enable you to connect to the Internet via one of their server computers, using a telephone number which they provide.

Your Windows Desktop probably already shows a number of Internet tools, as shown below.

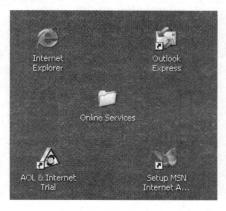

In the extract from the Microsoft Windows Desktop shown above, Internet Explorer and Outlook Express are respectively the Internet browser and e-mail programs included with Windows. AOL (America Online) is the "World's No.1" Internet Service Provider while MSN is Microsoft's own Internet Service.

Typically you pay for their services by a monthly or yearly subscription, although recently there was been a spate of "free" connection services. Some companies (like AOL, Freeserve and BT Internet) offer "unmetered" services which allow you to go online for as long as you like for one fixed monthly/yearly fee. To avoid receiving massive telephone bills, connection to the Internet must be available at the *local* telephone rate.

When you start to set up a connection to the Internet using Microsoft's Internet Connection Wizard, you are presented with a choice of companies. These fall into two categories, **Online Services** and **Internet Service Providers**.

Online Services are provided by companies such as AOL, and The Microsoft Network (MSN). In addition to giving you access to e-mail and the World Wide Web, the on-line services also provide their own extensive news and information pages.

You can see some of these companies by double clicking on the Online Services folder on the Windows desktop.

Some **Internet Service Providers (ISPs)** offer a specialist connection service to the Web, without the private news and information pages produced by the Online Services.

The Online Services also function as Information Service Providers (ISPs). Therefore, in general, future references to ISPs in this book should be taken to include the Online Services.

Many of the Internet Service Providers offer a free 30 day evaluation period, although you will normally have to provide your credit card details at the outset. You can often obtain CDs containing trial Internet connection software free on the front of magazines. Some of the larger players in the field such as America Online (AOL) and The Microsoft Network (MSN) may send you a CD in the post, if you have found your way onto their mailing list. You can also start the ball rolling by opening up the Online Services folder on your Windows desktop (as shown on the previous page) and double clicking on one of the icons.

Signing up for an Internet account is very easy, but you have to give your credit card details before the trial period begins. If you don't want to continue with the account, you must extricate yourself at the end of the trial period. The onus is on you to stop the subscription - otherwise your monthly payments will start automatically. It's a good idea, at the start, to note the arrangements for cancelling the account.

Until recently a number of companies were offering a "free" Internet connection service (not just for a limited trial period of 30 or 100 hours). Some of these services have since reverted to a monthly subscription, typically £14.99 a month.

Some criteria for choosing an Internet Service Provider might be:

- Speed and reliability when connecting to the Internet.
- Telephone access numbers available at *local* telephone rates.
- The monthly or yearly subscription charges.
- The number of e-mail addresses per account.
- The quality and cost of the telephone support service.
- Support for the latest technology (such as 56K V90 modems)
- In the case of Online Services providing content, the quality and quantity of the pages of information - news, sport, travel, weather, etc., and their value as a research and learning facility.
- Parental controls over children's access to inappropriate Web sites.
- Amount of Web space available for subscribers to create their own Web sites and any charges for this facility.

It's very easy to be confused by the large number of competing deals offered by the Internet Service Providers. A good source of help is the computing press, which regularly publishes helpful comparisons of the various ISPs and their charges.

Making the Connection

This section assumes your computer has Microsoft Windows installed and the modem is up and running. It is also assumed that you have set up an Internet browser such as Microsoft Internet Explorer or Netscape Navigator. There are several ways to launch the process of connecting to an Internet Service Provider or Online Service. Many of the services provide a free CD which just needs putting in the drive, then you follow the instructions on the screen. Or you can open up the **Online Services** folder on the Windows desktop and start the process by double clicking on a service.

Microsoft Windows provides the Internet Connection Wizard to simplify the process of connecting to the Internet. Double click the icon on the Windows Desktop, shown right, or select **Start**, **Programs**, **Accessories**, **Communications** and **Internet Connection Wizard**.

Apart from reminding you that your computer must be connected to the telephone line by a modem, you are given the choice of creating a new Internet account or transferring an old one. The third option includes a connection via a local area network and relates to Internet Connection Sharing by network client machines not fitted with their own modem.

If you choose to sign up for a new account, you will be connected to the Microsoft Internet Referral Service which presents you with a list of the available Internet Service Providers in your area.

Selecting one of these leads onto a sign-up process provided by the individual Internet Service Provider. This gives details not only of the monthly charges for the service but also any additional facilities provided. A telephone number is usually given, which can be used to cancel the account, if necessary, after the expiry of any free trial period. Whichever ISP you choose to subscribe to, you will be presented with dialogue boxes which require you to enter your personal details such as name, address, telephone number and the details of your credit card.

E-mail Addresses

When you sign up for an Internet account you will be able to choose, or be given, your own e-mail address. This is a unique location enabling your mail to reach you from anywhere in the world.

Common types of e-mail address are as follows:

stella@aol.com

james@msn.com

enquiries@wildlife.org.uk

The part of the address in front of the **@** sign is normally your *user* name or Internet *login* name. The second part of the address identifies the mail server at your company, organization or Internet Service Provider. The last part of the address is the type of organisation providing the service.

In the previous addresses **.com** refers to a commercial company. Other organisation types include:

    .edu   education

    .gov   U.S. government

    .org   non-profit making organisations

    .co   UK commercial company

Finally the e-mail address may end with a two digit code to denote the country, such as **uk** or **fr**.

Some Internet providers only allow you to have one e-mail address unless you open and pay for further accounts. However, there may be a time when you need more than one e-mail address, perhaps for different members of your family or to separate business and social correspondence. A number of companies offer free e-mail accounts - the only obvious drawback being that you may have to endure additional advertising. One of the well-known free e-mail services is Hotmail, operated by Microsoft and sponsored by advertising. This service is intended for people who are already paying for one e-mail account through their subscription to an Internet Service Provider or Online Service.

It is extremely easy to set up a new Hotmail account - just fill in a few personal details after logging on to the Web site at:

www.hotmail.com

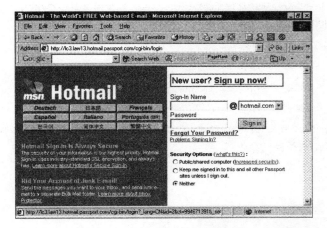

Hotmail is based on a World Wide Web site and uses your Internet browser rather than specialist e-mail software. Web-based e-mail provides easy access from remote locations anywhere in the world. You can also use Hotmail to read the e-mail you have received through your conventional e-mail accounts with other services.

Using Outlook Express

Outlook Express is the e-mail program provided as part of Microsoft Internet Explorer. It should have been installed when Windows was installed on your computer, but if not it can be added by selecting **Start**, **Settings**, **Control Panel** and **Add/Remove** programs. Select the **Windows Setup** tab and make sure there is a tick next to **Outlook Express.**

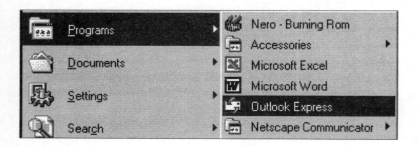

Once installed the program can be launched from **Start**, **Programs** and **Outlook Express** or from its icon on the Windows Desktop.

When the Outlook Express window opens, click the **New Mail** icon to start with a blank message as shown below.

When you first start Outlook Express it will try to connect you to the Internet. This is not necessary while you are composing a message, so to avoid connection charges click the **Work Offline** button. There is also a **Work Offline** option on the **File** menu.

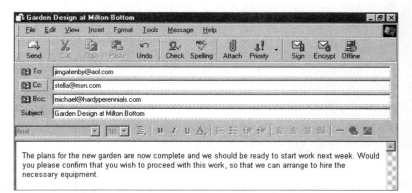

To:

Enter the e-mail address of your recipient in the **To:** slot. Selecting recipients for your e-mail from an electronic address book is discussed shortly.

Cc:

To send copies of the e-mail to additional recipients, list their e-mail addresses in the **Cc:** slot. In this method of sending multiple copies, everyone can see who else has received a copy of the message.

Bcc:

This slot doesn't appear until you select **View** and **All Headers** from the Outlook Express menus. If you place e-mail addresses in the **Bcc:** slot instead of the **Cc:** slot, recipients won't see who else has received a copy of the message.

Enter a meaningful title in the **Subject:** slot, so that the message can be easily identified at a later date. Then it's just a case of typing in your message. Notice that Outlook Express has many of the features of a word processor, with formatting options such as bold, italic, underline, bullets, numbering and justified text. The format menu also offers a full choice of fonts. There is a spelling checker and the very useful **Undo** button. The **Encrypt** feature is used to ensure that messages can only be read by the intended recipients.

Testing Your E-mail System

You can see whether your e-mail system is working by sending a short message to yourself.

- Working off-line, enter your own e-mail address in the **To:** slot.

- Enter a few words for the **Subject:**

- Type in a few lines of text and click **Send**.

You will probably see a small dialogue box saying that your message has been placed in your **Outbox** until the next time you select **Send/Recv** on the main Outlook Express menu as shown below. (To change between mailboxes, i.e. **Inbox**, **Outbox** and **Sent Items** click the icons shown in the left hand panel.)

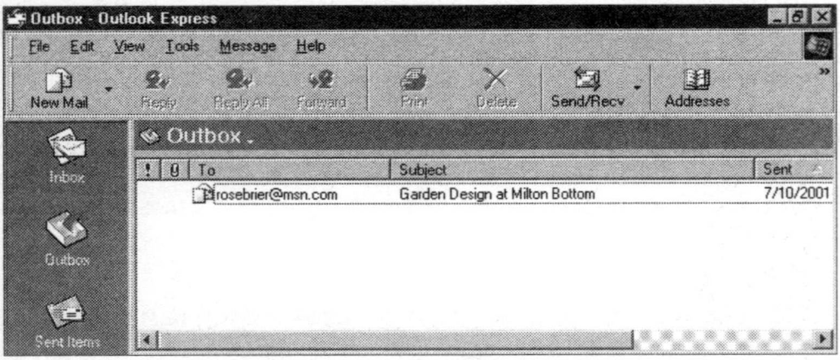

When you click **Send/Recv** you will be connected to the Internet and the message will be sent to the recipient's Internet Service provider's mail server. In this exercise, as you are sending the message to yourself, the message is sent to your own ISP's mail server.

When the message has been sent it is deleted from your **Outbox** and placed in the **Sent Items** mailbox as shown below.

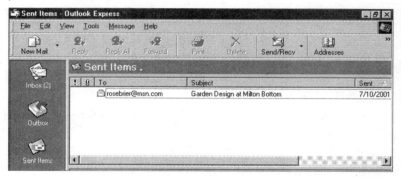

As the message was sent to your own e-mail address a copy should now be sitting in your **Inbox**, as shown below. (When the recipient is a person in another place, the message will be downloaded from their ISP's mail server to their computer next time they log on to the Internet to read their mail.)

Now you can open the e-mail to read by double clicking its entry in the **Inbox**. If necessary, make a hard copy using **File** and **Print**.

Dealing with Incoming E-mails

Once you have read the e-mails in your **Inbox**, there are several ways of dealing with them. If the e-mail is not important you will probably want to delete by highlighting it then pressing the **Delete** key. However, this

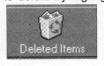

only sends them to the **Deleted Items** folder, located in the left panel of Outlook Express under the mailboxes. Mine is currently storing 400 old messages. To empty the **Deleted Items** folder,

select **Tools**, **Options...** and **Maintenance** and make sure **Empty messages from the 'Deleted Items' folder** is switched on, as shown below. Then click **Apply** and **OK**. As soon as you close Outlook Express, the **Deleted Items** folder will be cleared of messages.

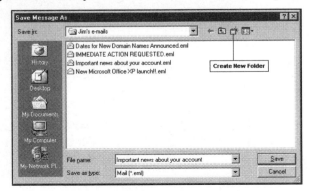

Saving Your E-mails

The e-mails you receive are automatically saved in your **Inbox**. However, this soon becomes cluttered and you'll probably want to store messages in folders of your own choice. E-mails can be saved in ordinary folders which you create, outside of the mailbox system.

From the **File** menu in Outlook Express, select **Save As...**. The **Save Message As** window appears, as shown on the previous page, allowing you to save the e-mails with a name of your choice in a folder of your choice. There is an icon which allows you to create new folders so that you can save your e-mails in folders under different headings or categories. The saved e-mails can be viewed later by double clicking on their name in the **Windows Explorer** or **My Computer**.

Responding to E-mails

Reply

To send a reply to an e-mail sitting in your **Inbox**, select the e-mail then click the **Reply** button. Also note **Reply All** and **Forward** below.

The Outlook Express message window opens up with the name or e-mail address of the sender of the e-mail already entered in the **To:** slot. (In this example I am replying to an e-mail I have sent myself). The **Subject:** slot is automatically infilled with the original subject, preceded by the letters **Re:**.

Note that the above reply also includes the text of the original message. This option can be switched off in the **Inbox** of Outlook Express after selecting **Tools**, **Options** and the **Send** tab. Then click the box next to **Include message in reply** to remove the tick, as shown below.

Options	? ☒

Spelling	Security	Connection	Maintenance
General	Read	Receipts	Send	Compose	Signatures

Sending

☑ Sa̲ve copy of sent messages in the 'Sent Items' folder

☑ Send messages i̲mmediately

☑ Automatically put people I reply to in my Address Bo̲ok

☑ A̲utomatically complete e-mail addresses when composing

☐ In̲clude message in reply

☑ R̲eply to messages using the format in which they were sent

International Settings...

Reply All

Choosing this option ensures that your reply is sent to all of the recipients of the original message, whose names or e-mail addresses are automatically infilled in the **To:** slot. Otherwise **Reply All** is similar to **Reply**, with the option to include the original message with your reply.

Forward

This option allows you to send a copy of an e-mail to one or more other people. Select the message to be forwarded then enter the e-mail name or addresses in the **To:** slot. Multiple e-mail addresses should be separated by a semi-colon (;). You can also enter a short message of your own to accompany the forwarded message. The **Subject:** slot will be infilled with the original subject, preceded by the letters **Fw:**.

Using the Address Book

This feature can be used to record all of your regular e-mail contacts. Instead of typing their e-mail address every time you send them a message, you simply select their name from the list in the address book.

The address book can be opened by clicking on its icon on the top of the Outlook Express window.

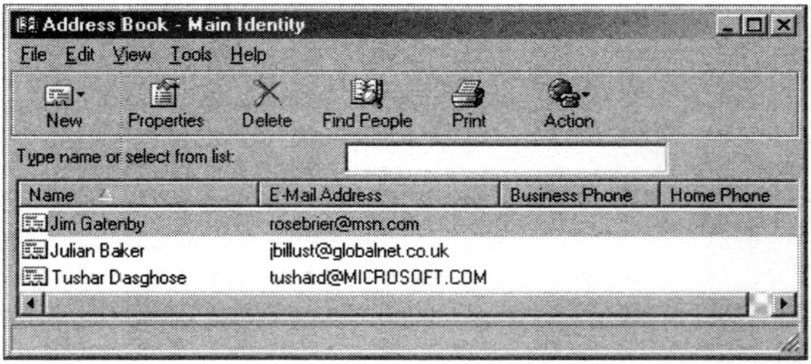

To make a new entry manually, click **New** as shown above and then type their details in the **Properties** window, shown below.

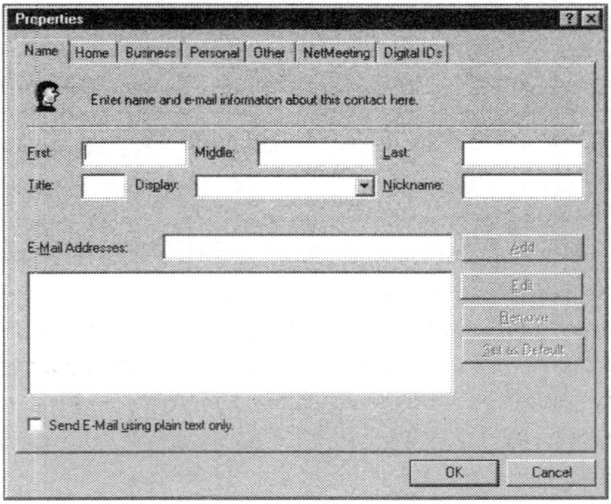

Adding Contacts to the Address Book

Apart from the contact's name and e-mail address, you can store a mass of other information such as their business details and a clickable link to their Web site, if a site exists.

New contacts can be added automatically to the address book, when you send a **Reply** to their e-mail. This option can be switched on or off in **Tools**, **Options...** and the **Send** tab.

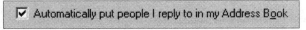

Senders of mail can be added to the address book by right-clicking their name in the **Inbox**. Then click **Add Sender to Address Book**.

Infilling Addresses into a New Message

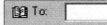

Instead of typing the e-mail address into the **To:** slot, click the book icon next to the word **To:**. This brings up the **Select Recipients** window. Select the names of the people you wish to receive the message, then click **To:** (or **Cc:** or **Bcc:**) to transfer them into the **Message recipients:** panel, below.

Clicking **OK** automatically places the selected contacts in the **To:** field (or **Cc:** or **Bcc:** fields, if applicable) of the new message.

E-mail Attachments

When you send an e-mail message, you can include with it an additional file known as an *attachment*. This can be any sort of file, usually selected from your hard disc. It could be, for example, a word processing document, graphics file, or photograph. As mentioned earlier, entire books (such as this one) can be sent as e-mail attachments. The process is relatively slow when using an ordinary modem, but still much faster than the traditional post.

Sending an E-mail Attachment

Attach

First the text of a new e-mail is entered in the normal way. Then click the **Attach** icon shown left or select **Insert** and **File Attachment...** from the menu bar.

> **Artwork for new book**
>
> File   Edit   View   Insert   Format   Tools   Message   Help
>
> Send   Cut   File Attachment...   Text from File   Picture   Horizontal Line   Check   Spelling   Attach   Priority   Sign   Encrypt   Offline
>
> To: rosebrie@
> Cc:
> Bcc:
> Subject: Artwork fo   My Business Card   Signature   Hyperlink
>
> Arial   10   B I U A
>
> Attached is the artwork you requested for the new book. If you double click the icon, the Paint program will be launched with the artwork file open. Then you can save the file on your hard disc in a directory of your choice.

The **Insert Attachment** box opens to allow you to select, from within the hierarchy of folders on your hard disc, the file to be attached to the e-mail. Clicking the **Attach** button inserts an **Attach:** field, an icon and file name for the attachment onto the

> Subject: Artwork for new book
> Attach: delphinium.bmp (37.5 KB)

e-mail, which is now ready to send. Now click **Send** and the message and its attached file will be sent as if they were a single entity. If you send a large file as an e-mail attachment, sending and receiving times will be substantially increased compared with text only messages.

Receiving an Attachment

When the message (together with the attachment) is received into an **Inbox**, the presence of the attachment is shown by a paperclip icon. This appears on the left of the entry for the message in the **Inbox**.

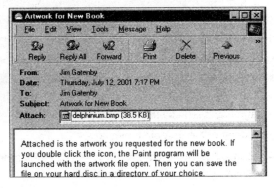

Double clicking the entry in the **Inbox** opens up the message together with the attachment as shown in the window below.

To view the attachment running in its own associated program (such as a bitmap program in Paint or a spreadsheet in Excel) double click the entry in the **Attach:** field. You will be given the chance to open the file immediately with a warning about the risk of viruses. Or you can save the file to your hard disc after selecting a suitable folder.

Any files you receive as e-mail attachments should be checked immediately using an up-to-date anti-virus program, like Norton AntiVirus or Dr. Solomon's Anti-Virus Toolkit.

Exercise 1: Sending and Receiving Electronic Mail

This exercise involves many of the skills required for the element "Use Electronic Mail for Business Communication" in the Internet Technologies Stage 1 course, from Oxford Cambridge and RSA Examinations. Ideally you need a contact who will send you an e-mail with an attachment and two more contacts who will acknowledge receipt of an e-mail. However, the **send**, **reply** and **forward** functions can all be practised using yourself as both sender and recipient.

1. Create a new message. The message is to be sent to two contacts of equal priority and copied to another. Their e-mail addresses should be retrieved from your address book.

2. Enter the text of the message and add your personal details.

3. Attach to the message a small file (text or graphics, etc.) which you have selected from your hard disc.

4. Send the message. Check that a copy of the outgoing message has been saved on your computer.

5. Print a copy of the outgoing message.

6. Ask a contact to send you an e-mail with an attachment. Open and read the e-mail and view the attachment.

7. Add the sender to the list of contacts in your address book.

8. Use the reply facility to inform the sender, with a short message, that you have received the e-mail. Add your personal details to the bottom of the message.

9. Use the forward facility to send a copy of the e-mail and its attachment to another contact. Include a short message and your personal details, together with the forwarded e-mail.

10. Save a copy of the incoming message (from 6. above) and its attached file in a folder outside of the mailbox system.

11. Delete the file from your mailbox.

12. Exit from the e-mail software using the correct procedure.

Checklist of Basic Internet Skills

This list is based on the Assessment Objectives of **Element 1: Use Electronic Mail for Business Communication**, from the Internet Technologies Stage 1 course, from Oxford Cambridge and RSA Examinations. You might wish to check your progress against this list and, if necessary, revisit any topics requiring further work.

Objective	Achieved
Create new e-mail message	☐
Use reply and forward facilities on incoming e-mail	☐
Send a message to multiple recipients	☐
Address outgoing messages using To:, Cc:, Bcc:	☐
Use an address book to store and retrieve address	☐
Store all outgoing messages	☐
Send messages	☐
Send, receive and access file attachments	☐
Access incoming messages	☐
Store incoming messages outside of mailboxes	☐
Store attachments outside of mailbox structure	☐
Delete messages	☐
Print all messages and attachments	☐
Exit the software following the correct procedure	☐

Retrieving Information from the Internet

Introduction

The World Wide Web is a collection of billions of pages of information covering every conceivable subject. A *web site* is a collection of related pages, belonging to an individual person or an organization. The Web pages are stored on many thousands of computers, known as Web *servers*, scattered all round the world. In order to retrieve information from the Web, we must first log on to the Internet and then connect to the Web server containing the relevant pages. A program called a *Web browser* is used to move about the Internet and to view and retrieve information. The most commonly used browsers are Microsoft Internet Explorer (part of Microsoft Windows) and Netscape Navigator, part of the Netscape Communicator suite of programs.

In some circumstances, it may be enough to simply view a Web page on our computer screen. Alternatively, all or part of the Web page can be downloaded from the Internet and stored on the hard disc of our own computer. Then the information can be viewed at any time in the future while working *offline*, i.e. without having to connect to the Internet.

If you find a Web page which you think may be useful in future, a link to the page can be saved as a *bookmark* or *favorite*. To return to the page at a later date, log on to the Internet and click the bookmark or favorite. This should connect your computer to the required Web page. Although bookmarks and favorites normally only save *links* to Web pages, rather than the content of the pages themselves, the **Favorites** feature in Internet Explorer has an option to allow a page to be viewed off-line.

Apart from viewing Web pages to research a particular subject, some Web pages enable programs i.e. software, to be downloaded and stored on your computer. This is now a common way of distributing software, often on a "try before you buy" basis, where you can use the program free for the first 30 days. Further use of the software requires a payment, the whole transaction being completed over the Internet. These topics are discussed in greater detail in the remainder of this chapter.

Connecting to a Web Site

One of the biggest problems with the Web is finding the information. The information is almost certainly out there somewhere, but how do we locate it? A key part of any Web page is the **URL** or **Uniform Resource Locator**. This is a unique address which identifies the page on the World Wide Web. For example,

http://www.mycompany.com

http:

Hypertext Transfer Protocol. This is the *protocol* or set of rules used by Web servers. Another popular protocol is **ftp** or File Transfer Protocol.

www

This means the Web site is part of the World Wide Web.

mycompany

This is the location of the Web server computer hosting the Web site. Usually a company or organization.

com

This denotes a Web site owned by a company. Other common *domains* are **edu** for education and **org** for non-profit making organizations.

An individual Web page within a Web site can be identified by adding its file name to the URL. For example:

http://www.mycompany.com/index.htm

index.htm or **index.html** is the name normally given to the Home Page on a Web site.

If you already know the URL of the required Web site, the task is relatively simple. For example, a company or organization will often give the address of its Web site on its stationery or advertising. Simply type the URL into the **Address** bar of Internet Explorer and click the **Go** button on the right.

On Netscape Navigator, the URL is entered into the **Location** bar, as shown below. After typing the address press **Enter**.

Both Internet Explorer and Netscape Navigator maintain lists of recently visited sites, which can be viewed by clicking the down arrow to the right of the **Address** or **Location** bar. Clicking an entry in the list returns you to the Web site. You can enter a URL while working off-line. On pressing **Enter** the browser will connect to the Internet and find the Web site.

If you don't know the address of the required Web page or site, then there are countless search tools available. These produce a list of Web sites which match the key words you typed in.

Using the Address Bar in Internet Explorer to Find Web Sites

Search tools, normally accessed via the **Search** button in your browser, are discussed in detail shortly. However, you can also carry out a search using the **Address** bar in Internet Explorer. Just type your key words into the **Address** bar and click **Go**. The results of the search can be presented in various ways, depending on the settings in **Tools**, **Internet Options** and **Advanced**, as shown below.

```
   Search from the Address bar
      When searching
         O  Display results, and go to the most likely site
         O  Do not search from the Address bar
         ⦿  Just display the results in the main window
         O  Just go to the most likely site
```

Searching the Internet

There are billions of pages of information stored on the World Wide Web. Whatever topic you want to find out about, no matter how obscure, someone is likely to have uploaded Web pages about it. In theory, this makes the Web the ideal tool for research on any subject under the sun. However, without a little knowledge about searching methods there can be frustration and wasted effort.

Suppose you have the pleasure of seeing a woodpecker in your garden and want to find out more about it. To search for information on the Web, we enter *key words or phrases* in a search program like **Google** shown below. Entering the key word **woodpecker** returns an unwieldy list of 152,000 Web pages, each containing the word woodpecker.

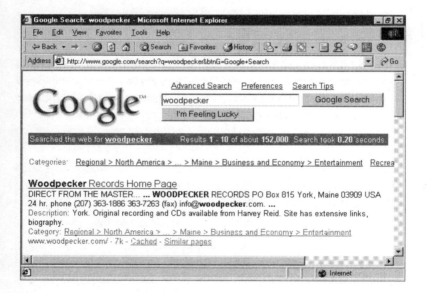

The problem is that by typing simply "woodpecker", we have found **152,000** pages where the word occurs, *in some context or other*, often in the name of some product being advertised.

Very many of the pages found have no relevance to our quest for information about the species of bird. We therefore need to find ways of refining the search to eliminate the irrelevant answers.

One strategy is to enter more key words, narrowing down the search. If, for example, **greater spotted woodpecker** is entered, the search tool finds a greatly reduced, but still massive, total of 13,200 results. This is because the search program finds all pages containing the key words *anywhere on the page*, not necessarily together or in the same order. So, for example, a page containing the irrelevant (in this context) **Heart-spotted Woodpecker, Greater Racquet-tailed and Bronzed Drongos** is also listed.

Untitled
... We came across one loose flock containing Heart-**spotted Woodpecker, Greater** Racquet-
and Bronzed Drongos, Asian Fairy Bluebird and Yellow-browed Bulbul. ...
www.ee.princeton.edu/~vivek/trips/Kerala99.html - 16k - Cached - Similar pages

---

In our bird example, we can narrow down the search much further by entering **"greater spotted woodpecker"**. The addition of the inverted commas ensures that only pages containing the key words *in the given order*, in the exact phrase, will be found. This modified search found only 269 (but highly relevant) results.

Google™

Advanced Search   Preferences   Search Tips

"greater spotted woodpecker"   Google Search

I'm Feeling Lucky

Searched the web for **"greater spotted woodpecker"**   Results 1 - **10** of about **269**. Search took **0.24** s

Greater-spotted woodpecker.
. **Greater-spotted woodpecker**.
www.bashedu.ru/konkurs/shakirova/foto/dyatel3_e.html - 1k - Cached - Similar pages

---

So you can see that quite minor "tweaks" to the search criteria i.e. key words, can drastically affect the quality and quantity of the results of a search. These issues are discussed in more detail later in this chapter.

Search Tools

Most of us start searching the Internet by clicking the **Search** button on a Web browser such as Internet Explorer or Netscape Navigator. On Internet Explorer, there is also a **Search the web** bar on the main Internet Explorer screen and **Search/On the Internet...** off the **Start** menu.

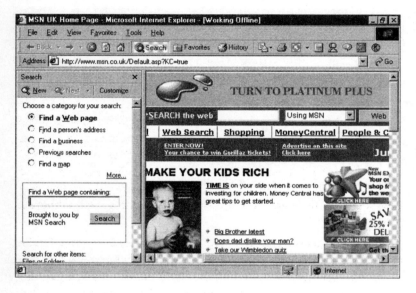

On the left-hand side you can choose to search in various categories such as addresses or businesses as well as simply for Web pages. Most of us would normally just enter our key word in the **Find a Web page containing:** slot, click the **Search** button and wait for the results. As mentioned earlier, we can greatly change the results of the search by modifying the key words entered, and this is discussed later.

There is also a lot more to searching than simply accepting the search tools presented to us by default by our browser. In fact, behind the **Search** button on your browser there is a whole battery of programs working to find the information you request from the Internet.

Most of these **search tools** are known as **search engines** while a few, although used in a similar way, are known as **directories**. You can see the search tools used by **MSN** by clicking **Customize** from the search window shown on the previous page.

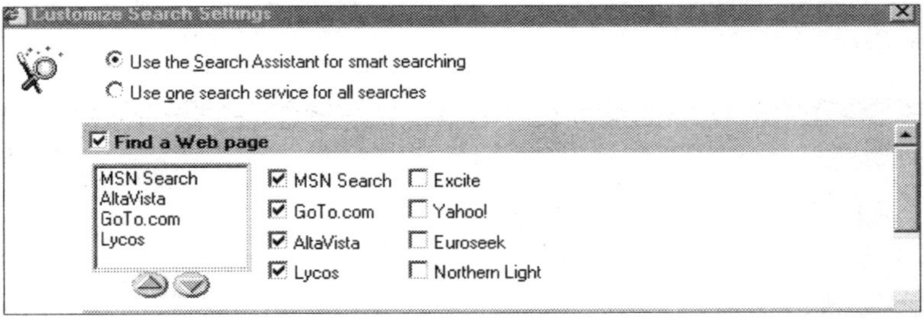

If you select **Use the Search Assistant...** as shown above, you can then choose a whole range of search tools by clicking to tick the adjacent squares. The point about using a battery of search tools is that if one doesn't find the required result, the others may - the search tools don't all work in the same way. It's possible, however, to confine your search to just one search tool by selecting **Use one search service...** as shown above.

Netscape also gives a choice of search tools, namely **Espotting**, **Excite** and **UK Plus** as shown below. Also note that **Netscape** displays a list of *categories*. Selecting a category, such as **Science**, ensures that any search is already confined to the right sphere. This reduces the number of irrelevant search results compared with an unrestricted search of the entire World Wide Web.

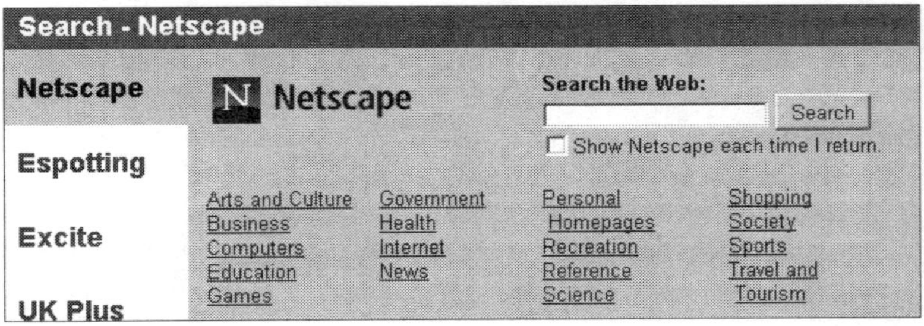

Search Engines and Directories

There are two main types of search tool, **Search Engines** and **Directories**. Although used in a similar way, they differ in the way they are created.

Search Engines

The search engine is an enormous index of millions of Web pages and their addresses. The index is created by a program known as a **robot**, **spider** or **crawler**. This visits every page and follows every link on a Web site, then copies the text of the pages to its index, along with the address details. This process is repeated at regular intervals to keep the index up-to-date. When you request a search of the Web, the search engine returns a list of the pages which match the search criteria. Clicking on a link in an entry in the results list calls up the Web page.

Well known search engines include Google, Excite, AltaVista, Lycos, HotBot, Ask Jeeves and Northern Light. Google is a very popular search engine which can be run from its search site at **www.google.co.uk**.

For more information and details of the vast number of alternative search engines, **www.searchenginewatch.com** is well worth a visit.

Directories

A directory is used to search for information in a similar way to a search engine. The difference is that a directory is compiled by a human, unlike the search engine index which is created by a computer. When a Web designer submits the details of their Web pages for inclusion in a directory, a short description is also provided. A human editor reviews the descriptions and then examines the Web sites. If considered suitable, the details of the Web site are included in the directory. Well known directories are Yahoo! and LookSmart.

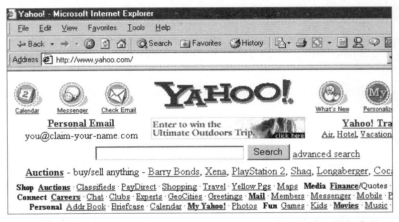

As shown above, in Yahoo!, you can enter key words in the search bar and click the **Search** button just as if you were using a search engine. However, a major difference with directories is that the information is arranged in *categories*, as shown in the following extract from the main Yahoo! screen.

With a directory you can follow down through the categories to narrow down your search. You can also enter a key word or phrase and search within a category. Although searching a directory yields less results than a search engine, the Web pages found should be highly relevant since you have already focused on the right category.

The various search engines might at first seem to be separate entities produced by different organizations. However, there are all sorts of associations and alliances in operation. So that although you type your query into one particular search engine or directory, the answers may be provided by an entirely different search tool.

At the end of a list of Yahoo! search results there are links to some of the major search engines, shown below under **Other Search Engines**. These should increase the success of the search.

The reason for these alliances is that the search engine and directory companies make their living from the advertisements which decorate their pages. In order to attract advertising, the search engines and directories must be able to prove that they are heavily used, i.e. they receive large numbers of "hits" or visits from people browsing the Web. To increase their presence on the Web and therefore the number of hits, the companies behind the search engines and directories pay large sums to other companies willing to include links to their search engines or directories.

Copernic 2001: A Search Agent

A search agent is a program which uses a battery of search tools to find what you are looking for. **Copernic 2001 Basic** is part of a family of software which also includes **Copernic 2001** and **Copernic 2001 Pro**. The Basic version is free and, unusually, there is no time limit. To download a copy of Copernic, log on to the Web site at:

http://www.copernic.com

When you have downloaded and installed the software (as discussed elsewhere in this book), it can be launched from its icon on the desktop. Clicking on **Search** in the main Copernic window (shown on the next page) allows you to enter your key words or a question. Alternatively the search can match the exact phrase, search for all words (occurring anywhere on the page) or simply find pages which contain at least one of the words.

You can also choose to search the entire Web or confine your search within a list of categories, obtained by clicking the down arrow to the right of **Category** in the **New Search** window shown on the previous page.

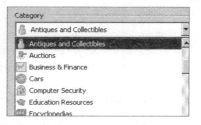

After you click **Search Now** you are informed of the search progress as Copernic puts each of the search engines to work.

At the end of the search the results are shown in the Copernic window with the key words highlighted in yellow.

Title	Address	Score	Searcl
USA Flags	http://www.usaflags.net/		Open
American flags, Betsy Ross flag, and other items such as American Bald Eagle statues and wall clocks featuring the American flag.			
U.S.S.T. Home Page	http://www.usstock.com/		AltaVi
Click HERE for a text only. version of this page. U. S. Stock Transfer Corporation. [Home] [What's New] [Search] [Mission] [Feedback] (text links...			
The north american bald eagle	http://tx.essortm.../northamericanb_rmla.htm		Open
An article about the North American bald eagle, including where these eagles are located, their nests, food, habits,			

A page is ranked according to the frequency of the key words on the Web page and the number of search engines which found it. Clicking on a result launches the required Web page in your browser.

Searching with Google

Google is a popular search engine developed by Stanford University. It is fast and powerful yet easy to use. To start using Google, log on to the Web site at **Google.co.uk** or **Google.com**.

As shown above, you can add a **Google** toolbar to Internet Explorer. To start a search, simply type your key words in the search bar then press **Enter** or click the **Google Search** button. To go straight to the first Web page returned by **Google**, click **I'm Feeling Lucky**. Notice also that you can choose to search the entire Web or search only pages from the UK.

As mentioned earlier, the search can be greatly affected by the number of key words entered and there are various other techniques which have the effect of narrowing down or widening the scope of a search. These are discussed shortly, but for the time being we'll look at a search for the popular "classic" car from the sixties, the Austin Mini Cooper. Although I have entered **"austin mini cooper"**, the same results will be obtained whether you use upper or lower case letters or a mixture of both.

When the previous search was carried out using Google, 1,560 results were returned in no time at all - the actual search took only 0.69 seconds, as shown across the top of the results list below.

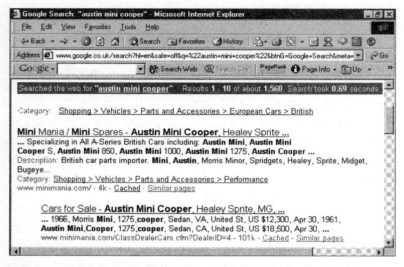

Notice that each entry starts with one line of underlined text. This is the page title; clicking in this line opens up the Web page. The text underneath the title is an extract from the actual Web page, with the key words shown bold. At various places in the results list, *categories* are listed which link to further information which may be relevant.

In the above example, **www.minimania.com/** is the URL or Web address of the first search result. When two or more pages from the same Web site are included in the results, the most relevant result is listed first, followed by the other results from the same site, shown *indented*.

4k (4 kilobytes) in the first result refers to the amount of text in the corresponding Web page.

In Google, pages are ranked (i.e. placed near the top of the results list) based on several criteria. A page with many links to it from other pages is considered to be important and ranked highly.

Cached Pages

In order to compile its index, the Google search engine "crawls" a Web site and makes a copy of every page, which is stored in a "cache". Clicking the title line in a results list should lead you to the Web page. If for any reason the actual Web page is not accessible, you can retrieve the crawler copy from the search engine cache. Click on the word **Cached** in the relevant entry in the results list. The cached pages may not be the same as the latest Web pages but they might still be helpful.

Advanced Searching with Google

There is a link to set up more precise searches on the main Google window. Click the words **Advanced Search** as shown below.

The **Advanced Web Search** window appears, allowing you to specify the way Google will match Web pages with the key words you have entered as your search criteria.

There is a choice of languages for the returned Web pages and an option to specify where your key words should appear on the page, e.g. in the title. Google can restrict a search to a particular Web site or domain, or exclude a site from the search. The **SafeSearch** filter is used to exclude sites which may be considered unsuitable for children.

The Basics of Searching

Although there are some differences between individual search engines,
there is a set of basic rules of searching which generally apply. Precise
details of which commands apply to which search engines can be found
at **http://searchenginewatch.com/** in the feature entitled "Search
Engine Features For Searchers". The following pages gives an overview
of some of the most common commands. When entering the key words
in the search bar on your browser, there is no need to worry about
upper or lower case letters. All search criteria are treated as lower case
and the results are not case sensitive - in the example below, pages
containing **austin mini**, **Austin Mini** or even **AUSTIN MINI** would be
returned.

Using the + Sign to Include Terms

To make sure a word or term (such as a single character or single digit)
is present in any results pages, precede the term with a space and the **+**
sign when entering the search criteria.

| +austin +mini | **Search** |

The list of results will include all pages found with both the words **austin**
and **mini** *somewhere within the page*. The two words need not be
together on the page, or in the same order.

Searched the web for **austin mini**.   Results **1 - 10** of about **161,000**

If you were only interested in cars which had been prepared for racing,
you could narrow down the search by adding an extra key word:

| +austin +mini +racing | **Search** |

Web pages will be listed in the results which contain all three words in
any order, somewhere on the page.

Searched the web for **+austin +mini +racing**   Results **1 - 10** of about **14,600**

Using the - Sign to Exclude Terms

In the previous example, many of the pages found will refer to the popular Austin Mini Cooper. Suppose we want to find all ordinary Austin Minis which are not the high perfomance Cooper model. This would be achieved by preceding the word **cooper** with a - sign.

| +austin +mini -cooper | | Search |

The results of the search would exclude all Web pages containing the word **cooper** anywhere on the page.

Searched the web for +austin +mini -cooper   Results 1 - 10 of about 141,000.

Phrase Search Using " "

The addition of inverted commas (quotation marks or speech marks) around the search criteria means that only Web pages containing the *exact phrase*, i.e. all of the words *in the same order*, will be listed in the results.

| "austin mini cooper" | | Search |

Searched the web for "austin mini cooper"   Results 1 - 10 of about 1,420.

Please note that, in this example, **"austin mini cooper"** only yields a relatively small number of search results. Entering the search criteria as **+austin +mini +cooper** yields far more results because this will find Web pages containing the three words *anywhere* on the page, not necessarily in close proximity. You can also combine search criteria as follows, to include only cars painted in British Racing Green.

| "austin mini cooper" +"british racing green" | | Search |

With such a tight specification for the search criteria it's perhaps not surprising that only 4 (but highly relevant) results were found.

Searched the web for "austin mini cooper" +"british racing green"   Results 1 - 4 of 4.

Bookmarks and Favorites

When you have found a page you are interested in, either by entering its URL in the Address Bar or as a result of a search, you can save a link to the page, for future reference. This saves repeating a search later on.

In Netscape Navigator the saved links are known as *bookmarks*, while Internet Explorer uses the American word *favorites*. You can also save the *list of results of a search*, as discussed shortly.

Bookmarks in Netscape Navigator

In Netscape Navigator, with the required Web page displayed on the screen, click **Bookmarks** off the menu, as shown below.

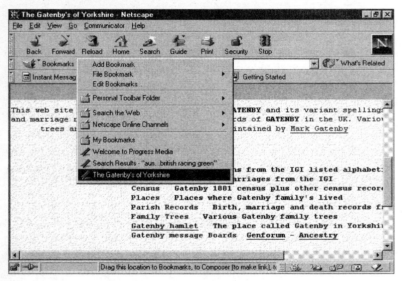

Now you select **Add Bookmark** from the menu shown above. The title of the Web page is added to the bottom of the list under **My Bookmarks**. The above menu also has an **Edit Bookmarks...** option. This allows you to delete bookmarks or organize them into folders.

Whenever you are connected to the Internet in future, any Web page which has been previously visited (and saved as a bookmark) can be accessed on-line. Simply click its entry in the list of bookmarks.

Favorites in Internet Explorer

To save a link to a Web page in Internet Explorer, select **Favorites** and **Add to Favorites...** off the menu. By default, the title of the Web page appears in the **Name:** bar. As shown in the **Add Favorite** dialogue box below, the default name can be replaced with a name of your choice.

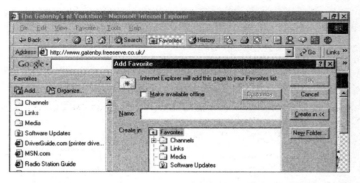

Favorites can be saved in different folders using **Create in <<** and there is a button to create a new folder. Switching on **Make available offline** allows you to view pages later, when not connected to the Internet.

The **Favorites window** has an option to **Organise...** favorites. This enables entries in the favorites list to be arranged in folders and deleted or renamed, as shown below.

Whenever you are connected to the Internet in future, any Web page which has been previously visited (and saved as a favorite) can be accessed on-line (or offline if this option was switched on when the favorite was created). Simply click its entry in the list of favorites.

Saving a Search

When a search is complete and the results are presented as a list, you can save the search site and the list of results. In Internet Explorer click **Favorites** and **Add to Favorites....** On Netscape Navigator use **Bookmarks** and **Add Bookmark**. This enables you to recall the search site and the list of search results, at some future date.

Retrieving the Results List of a Previous Search

On Internet Explorer, click on the entry for the search site in the **Favorites** panel on the left-hand side of the window shown above. This brings up the list of results from the search done at a previous time.

On Netscape Navigator, select **Bookmarks** and click **Search Results**.

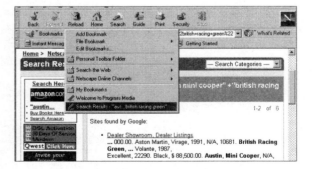

Clicking on an underlined title in the results list in the right-hand panel (shown in both screenshots above) will take you to the corresponding Web page.

The History Feature

Apart from **Favorites** in Internet Explorer and **Bookmarks** in Netscape Navigator, links to visited sites are also saved automatically. This is done by a **History** feature in both Internet Explorer and Netscape.

Internet Explorer has a **History** button, which leads to a list of links to recently visited sites, in a panel on the left of the Explorer window.

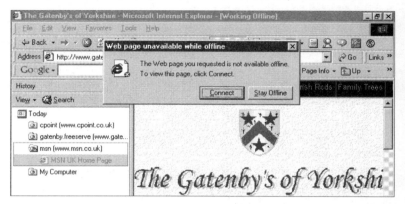

If you click one of the entries in the **History** panel, you will be connected to the corresponding Web page. You may need to click the **Connect** button, as shown above, if you are not already on-line to the Internet.

You can set the number of days for which links are kept and also clear all entries from **History**. To access these features in Internet Explorer select **Tools** and **Internet Options...** and the **General** tab.

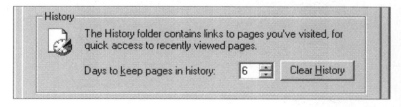

In Netscape Navigator the **History** list appears after selecting **Communicator**, **Tools** and **History**. Settings for the number of days to keep pages and a **Clear History** button are accessed from **Edit** and **Preferences...**.

Saving Information from Web Pages

Previous pages in this chapter discussed the way the *links* to Web pages can be saved using Favorites or Bookmarks. These allow you to log on to the Internet and reconnect to a Web site visited previously. It is also possible, when saving Favorites, to make a page available offline. This means the page can be viewed in Internet Explorer at a later date, without connecting to the Internet.

Copies of complete Web pages or just parts of them can also be saved on your hard disc. The information saved on your hard disc can be used in various ways. For example:

- Copy and paste the information into a word processing document, as part of a report or presentation. (While respecting any copyright issues.)

- Send a Web a page to a friend or colleague as an e-mail attachment.

- Print a copy of the information on paper to show other people, away from the computer.

Saving a Web Page to Your Hard Disc

When you are connected to the Internet, with the required page displayed on the screen in Internet Explorer, select **File** and **Save As....**

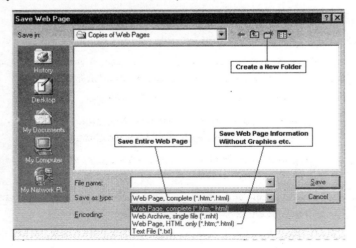

Before saving a Web page, it's often a good idea to create a new folder, using the icon in the **Save Web Page** dialogue box shown on the previous page. Then enter a name for the file and select from one of several file formats in **Save as type**:. These file types include:

Web Page, complete (*.htm, *.html)

This format saves everything on the page i.e. text, graphics files and any sound files, etc.

Web Archive, single file (*.mht)

This takes a snapshot of the Web page and saves it as a single file.

Web Page, HTML only (*.htm, *.html)

This option saves only the text, in HTML format.

Web pages saved in the above formats can be viewed off-line at a later date, in a browser such as Internet Explorer or Netscape Navigator. (The browser can be set to work off-line using the main **File** menu.)

Text File (*.txt)

This is plain text without any of the formatting features built into pages in the HTML language. A **Text File** is universally acceptable to other programs such as word processors and simple text editors like Windows Notepad and WordPad.

Netscape Navigator also uses **File** and **Save As...** to save complete Web pages for viewing off-line.

Saving Part of a Web Page

If you only want to copy say a piece of text from a Web page, a simple method (in both Internet Explorer and Netscape Navigator) is:

- Select the required text on the Web page.

- Click **Edit** and select **Copy** from the menu. This puts a copy of the piece of text onto the Windows Clipboard.

- Open the destination for the Web page extract. This might be a Microsoft Word document, for example.

- Select **Edit** and **Paste** to place the Web page extract onto the page in the document, which can now be saved.

Saving a Graphic Image from a Web page

While connected on-line to the Internet, with your browser (e.g. Internet Explorer or Netscape Navigator) displaying the required Web page:

- Right click over the image to be saved. A menu appears including the option to save the picture in a folder of your choice. There are also options to create a shortcut from the Windows Desktop to the Web page or to use the picture as Windows Wallpaper.

- Select **Save Picture As:...** from the menu which appears, as shown above. This leads to the **Save Picture** dialogue box. Here you can enter a name for the picture and choose whether to save it in the **.bmp** or **.jpeg** formats (discussed elsewhere in this book).

- The picture can now be opened for viewing off-line. Both **.bmp** and **.jpeg** files can be opened in Paint, which is supplied as a free accessory to Microsoft Windows. You might also use the highly rated PaintShop Pro image editing software to view and possibly modify an image copied from the Internet. A copy of the graphic image can easily be printed using **File** and **Print...** from the graphics program.

Printing a Web Page

Both Internet Explorer and Netscape Navigator have options to print Web pages. From the menu select **File** and **Print...**. There is also a **Print Preview...** option showing how the pages will print on paper.

Some Web pages print perfectly while you are on-line to the Internet, while others miss out important information. If you have problems printing while on-line, try some of the methods described on the previous pages for saving information from Web pages to your hard disc. For example, select all or part of a page then use **Edit** and **Copy** in the browser to place the information on the clipboard, before using **Edit** and **Paste** to put the Web information into a word processor like Microsoft Word. Then the information can be printed like any other word processing document.

Downloading Software From The Internet

It's not always essential to travel to a shop or contact a mail order company to obtain software. Although many programs are still sold on CDs in boxed packages, there's a huge amount of software available over the Internet. This is delivered to your hard disc through the telephone lines or whatever medium connects your computer to the Internet. Much of this software is known as "try before you buy"; a fully working copy is downloaded to your machine but the program only works for an evaluation period of 30 days, typically. After this time you must make a payment to continue to use the software. Many of the well-known software packages can be evaluated and purchased in this way. These include the latest versions of Web browsers like Internet Explorer and Netscape Navigator. A site containing a large number of programs for downloading is the Shareware Web site at:

http://shareware.cnet.com/

Some programs are initially free, but users may be asked to make a voluntary donation after evaluating the software. Other programs are completely free, but do not provide all of the features of a fully working and paid for copy. Essential features like printing may be missing.

For example, you may be able to download a demonstration version of a desktop publishing program. This may allow you to create a document on screen but will not allow the document to be printed on paper.

The main disadvantage of downloading software using a typical modem and telephone line is that large programs can take several hours to download. Software is transmitted in a highly compressed format in order to save time. Compression is achieved using software like PKZIP and WinZip. These strip out commonly occurring words and features in a file (such as "the") and replace them with a more compact code.

WinZip is an invaluable tool for creating compressed files (known as ZIP files) for speedy transmission over the Internet, for example as e-mail attachments. It can also be used to "decompress" or *extract* the files at the receiving end. An evaluation copy of WinZip is available from:

http://www.winzip.com/

An important feature of WinZip is the ability to create *self-extracting* compressed files. This means the ZIP files can be "unzipped" from their compressed format to a fully working format, simply by double clicking on the file name after downloading the file from the Internet. Self-extracting files have the **.exe** extension after the file name.

The Download Process

The main steps in downloading software from the Internet are:

- Connect to the Web site which contains the software, locate the **Download** section and select the required software.

- If necessary, select the download location from a choice of servers around the world.

- Click the **Download** button to start transferring a copy of the program (in its compressed format) to your hard disc.

- If the downloaded program saved on your hard disc is an **.exe** file, double click the file name in Windows Explorer or My Computer to install the software on your computer. The program should now be fully operational. If the downloaded program is a ZIP file, it will need to be unzipped using a program like WinZip, before running the installation program.

Downloading a Copy of Copernic 2001

As mentioned earlier in this chapter, Copernic 2001 is a popular search agent. A *search agent* is a program which uses a whole battery of *search engines* to carry out a search of the World Wide Web. There is a family of Copernic 2001 programs and the Basic version is available free. Unusually, there is no time limit, unlike a lot of software where there's a charge for continued use after an initial 30 day trial period. Copernic 2001 must copied from the Internet and installed on your own hard disc, where it can be launched from the **Start/Programs** menu or by double clicking its desktop icon.

To connect to the Copernic Web site enter **http://www.copernic.com/** in the address or location bar of your Web browser. (In general, if you don't know the complete address of the Web site, simply type in the name of the company or organization into the address bar. A browser like Internet Explorer should find the site for you).

From the Copernic 2001 Home Page, select **Downloads**. This leads to the **Downloads** window shown below, from where you can select the version of Copernic 2001 and start the process by clicking **Download Now!**

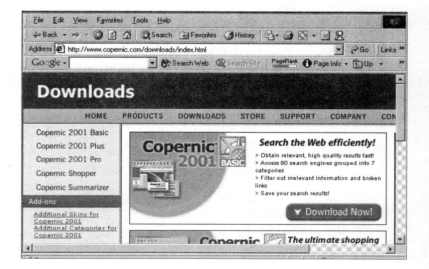

Before starting the actual download, you are presented with a list of options, such as the ability to reject advertising banners and to select

English as the language. Now click the **Download** button for Copernic 2001 Basic, which appears under *FREE!* as shown on the left. A dialogue box appears from which you choose **Save this program to disk**. On clicking **OK** you are given the chance to specify the destination folder for the downloaded Copernic Basic 2001 file. In this example, shown below, I have selected **C:\My Download Files** as the destination.

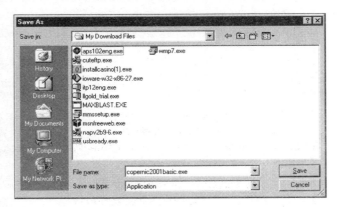

At this stage you can, if you wish, create a new folder into which the downloaded file can be saved. The **Create New Folder** icon is the

middle one shown on the left and in the **Save As** window shown above. Please note that the file about to be downloaded, **copernic2001basic.exe** is a self-extracting compressed file. This is the *installation* program which will be used to set up a working version of Copernic 2001 Basic. If you keep the **.exe** file on your hard disc, you can always repeat the installation at a later date, should the original installation of the program become damaged.

In the above folder you can see a lot of other downloaded **.exe** files. For example, **cuteftp.exe** is the installation program for the CuteFTP File Transfer Protocol program mentioned elsewhere in this book. **wmp7.exe** is the installation program for the Windows Media Player.

When you click **Save** the download process starts and you are informed of progress by the window shown below.

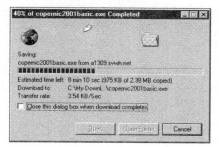

Notice that the progress window above gives the name of the **.exe** file, in this case **copernic2001basic.exe** and the destination folder, **C:\My Downloads**. In some downloads, the names will be quite obscure and it may be worth writing them down for future reference.

When the download is complete, the **.exe** file will be saved on your hard disc. You can select either **Open** or **Open Folder** if you want to start the installation of Copernic 2001 immediately. Alternatively click **Close** to do the installation later.

To install the new software from the **.exe** file, open the download folder in My Computer or the Windows Explorer

Address 🗀 C:\My Download Files				
Name	Size	Type	Modified ▽	
🗐 copernic2001basic.exe	2,446 KB	Application	7/3/2001 9:16 AM	
🗐 ff THE EVIDENCE.PPT	107 KB	Microsoft PowerPoin...	6/29/2001 9:10 AM	
🗐 520.pdf	135 KB	Adobe Acrobat Doc...	6/21/2001 12:07 PM	
🗐 katalog-00-01.pdf.realdo...	38 KB	REALDOWNLOAD ...	6/21/2001 12:06 PM	

To start the installation process, double click the name of the **.exe** file, in this case **copernic2001basic.exe**. From now on, installation of the software proceeds in the normal way, requiring you to accept certain Licence Agreements and to click **Next** between stages.

Finally you should have a working version of the software, Copernic 2001 Basic in this example, which can be launched from the **Start/Programs** menu or from its icon on the Windows Desktop, shown right.

Exercise 2: Retrieving Information from the Internet

(This exercise involves the skills required for the element "Use the Internet for On-Line Research" in the Internet Technologies Stage 1 course, from Oxford Cambridge and RSA Examinations.)

Look in a newspaper, magazine or on packaging, etc., and notice how many companies list their own Web site address. Note the Web address (or URL) of a large organization. The address should be something like **www.entrepreneurs.co.uk/**.

1.   Enter the URL you have found into the address or location bar in your Web browser and connect to the home page of the company. Follow one of the links to another page within the Web site and mark the page using the bookmark or favorite facility on your browser.

You are required to find out about **growing hardy perennials**.

2.   Use a web-based search engine to find a web page that contains the relevant information in the form of text.

Mark the page using the bookmark or favorite facility on your browser.

Print a copy of the page containing the information.

You need to find out about current **UK Monthly Rainfall**

3.   Use a Web-based search engine to find a page containing the **UK Monthly Rainfall** in the form of a table or set of numbers.

Mark the page using the bookmark or favorite facility on your browser.

Print a copy of the page containing the table of figures.

4.   Use a Web-based search engine to find a page containing the **UK Monthly Rainfall** in the form of a graph.

Mark the page using the bookmark or favorite facility on your browser.

Print a copy of the page containing the graph.

You need to obtain details of a book on the cultivation of **delphiniums**.

5. Access the Web site of one of the major on-line booksellers.

    Use the *local* search facilities to locate a Web page displaying details of a book containing the appropriate information.

    Mark the page using the bookmark or favorite facility on your browser.

    Print a copy of the page containing the book details.

You need to find out further information about the company whose Web site you accessed in question 1.

6. Recall the bookmark or favorite for the company and follow a link to a new page of information.

    Mark the page using the bookmark or favorite facility on your browser.

    Print a copy of the page containing the information.

7. Access your Web browser's bookmark or favorites facility and check the list of stored URLs. If possible make a printout of this list.

8. Exit from the Web browser following the correct procedures.

Checklist of Basic Internet Skills

This list follows closely the Assessment Objectives of **Element 2: Use the Internet for On-line Research**, from the Internet Technologies Stage 1 course, from Oxford Cambridge and RSA Examinations. You might wish to check your progress against this list and, if necessary, revisit any topics requiring further work.

Objective	Achieved
Navigate the World Wide Web using hyperlinks	☐
Access specified remote Web pages.	☐
Store URLs in an appropriate facility	☐
Access a Web page from a stored URL	☐
Use a general Web search engine	☐
Use internal search engine from specified Web site	☐
Retrieve a Web page containing specified text	☐
Retrieve a Web page containing specified numbers	☐
Retrieve a Web page containing a graph	☐
Print Web pages ensuring the content is relevant	☐
Exit the software using the correct procedure.	☐

Creating a Web Site:
An Overview

Introduction

A Web site consists of one or more pages of information stored centrally on a special computer known as an Internet *server*, allowing access by millions of people. Web pages usually contain text and pictures but may also include other features such as links to other pages, buttons, menus, order forms, sound recordings, animations and video clips.

Internet Server

The Web server is a powerful computer located at the premises of an Internet Service Provider (ISP) - the company that provides your connection to the Internet, usually at the cost of a monthly subscription. Well known Internet Service Providers include AOL and The Microsoft Network. The Internet Service Provider usually offers its own information service, consisting of pages of news and topical information. The ISP also provides a gateway to the World Wide Web with its millions of pages covering virtually every subject under the sun.

The ISP should also allow you some space on one of its servers, on which to store your own Web pages. While you are developing your Web site, all of the new pages should be saved locally on the hard disc inside of your computer, normally the **C:** drive. When the Web site is complete, all of the files can be *uploaded* and saved on the server of the company hosting your Web site, frequently the Internet Service Provider.

Web Browser

The Web browser is a program installed on all computers connected to the Internet, on which you can search the Internet and display Web pages. Two of the most well known Web browsers are Microsoft Internet Explorer and Netscape Navigator.

Links

An important feature of all Web sites is the ability to move between pages by clicking on special highlighted text, known as *hyperlinks*. These links enable the user to switch to different pages within the same

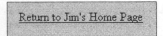

Web site or to look at a completely different Web site, perhaps on a server in another part of the world.

Finding a Web Page: The Uniform Resource Locator

Each Web site has a unique address which enables a Web site to be found on the Internet. This address is known as the **Uniform Resource Locator (URL)**. To move to a particular site, the URL is entered into the **Address** bar of a Web browser, as shown below.

Web Page Content

Web sites are created by a diverse range of people for a variety of purposes. Someone might want to make information available to others who share a common interest such as a sport or a hobby. A large company or organization may use a Web site to promote its products and services or recruit staff world-wide.

Companies may also create a private information network, known as an *intranet.* This is similar to the Web but the pages are accessible only to users within the organization.

A major advantage of using the World Wide Web to publish information is that facts and figures can be updated more quickly and easily than material printed by traditional methods in books and brochures. The Web can therefore be used to provide *up-to-date information* on national emergencies such as the recent epidemic of foot and mouth disease or the latest results of medical research. High quality information including graphs, maps, statistics and diagrams can be viewed on the screen or printed on paper.

Another advantage of Web pages available over the Internet is that they can be *interactive.* For example, it's easy to provide a link on screen to enable the "surfer" to send an e-mail to a particular address, to fill in questionnaires on-line or to download software, videos and music.

The Web sites of e-commerce companies such as Amazon.co.uk allow you to order goods quickly and easily over the Internet with just a single click of the mouse.

Design Considerations

Before starting work on producing a Web site, it's a good idea to sketch out a plan of each page, using pencil and appear. This will include the layout of text and pictures. If your site involves lots of individual pages connected by hyperlinks, then a plan showing the way they are to be linked will be useful.

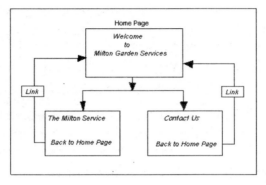

When inserting graphics into a Web page, some caution is needed. Large graphics consume huge amounts of memory and take ages to load. This is very off-putting for anyone waiting to view your Web site. Some strategies are available to help with this problem and the subject is discussed in more detail in the next two chapters.

As with similar activities like Desktop Publishing, the tendency is for novices to use every feature available. This may produce a document which is too "busy", with an excess of different fonts, colours and graphics. The expression "less is more" is particularly appropriate in this context.

A good strategy is to look at some existing Web sites aimed at a similar target audience to yours. It's illegal to copy actual material such as graphics and then insert them on your Web site. However, you can safely look at other sites for inspiration and for general ideas about style, layout and the use of text and background colours.

Working With HTML

Web pages are written in a language called HTML (HyperText Markup Language), discussed in detail in the next chapter. A page of HTML coding can look very complicated, but it's really just simple instructions to control the layout of the text and graphics on the Web page. In the example below a piece of text is centred and formatted as a large heading. **<h1>** is a *tag* which specifies the heading in a large font size.

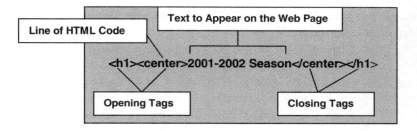

Viewing the HTML Code of Existing Pages

The HTML coding used to produce existing Web pages can be viewed from the browser software. With a Web page open in Internet Explorer select **View** and **Source** from the menus. In Netscape Navigator use **View** and **Page Source**. From Internet Explorer, the HTML code for the page is displayed in the Notepad text editor, in front of the Web page.

Methods of Creating Web Pages

There are various alternative ways to produce the HTML code for a Web page:

Method 1: Using a Text Editor to Produce HTML Code

This method is relatively hard work and time consuming, since you have to learn the commands of a simple language (discussed later). You must also type all of the tags (such as **<h1>** and **<center>**) as well as the page content itself. However, it's cheap since there's no need to buy expensive software and install it on your hard disc. A simple text editor like Microsoft Notepad is all you need and this is provided free with Microsoft Windows. If you understand HTML coding you will be able to tweak the coding produced by an HTML editor. This may be necessary to solve problems and achieve results which the dedicated Web design software cannot. The finished page is saved with the **.htm** or **.html** file name extension.

Method 2: Using A Word Processor to Produce HTML Code

Using a word processor like Microsoft Word, Corel WordPerfect or Lotus WordPro, simply enter and lay out the page as if it's a normal word processor document. Then select **Save as type: Web Page (*.htm: *.html)** from the list of file types, as shown below.

	Word Document (*.doc)
	Web Page (*.htm; *.html)
Page title:	Document Template (*.dot)
	Rich Text Format (*.rtf)
File name:	Text Only (*.txt)
	Text Only with Line Breaks (*.txt)
Save as type:	Web Page (*.htm; *.html)

The word processing document is converted to HTML code by the software, so there's no need for you to know how to write the code. The word processor allows you to produce Web pages easily and cheaply, since most computers already have a word processing package installed. However, this method lacks many of the facilities of HTML editors such as Microsoft FrontPage or Macromedia DreamWeaver.

Method 3: Using an HTML Editor to Produce HTML Code

Well known HTML editors include Macromedia DreamWeaver, Adobe
GoLive, Adobe PageMill and Microsoft FrontPage. Internet Explorer
includes a free HTML editor called FrontPage Express and there is a
more powerful professional version, Microsoft FrontPage. This program
is included with Microsoft Office 2000 Premium Edition and can also be
bought separately. For users of Microsoft Office, FrontPage has the
advantage of a similar "look and feel" to programs like Microsoft Word,
making FrontPage relatively easy to learn.

When using an HTML editor i.e. Web design program, you simply type
out your Web pages as if you were using a word processor and the
editor produces all of the HTML code for you. This includes the ability to
insert powerful features such as colour, sound, music, animations and
video clips, plus menus, buttons, links and tables. Ready-made
templates allow professional-looking pages rich in features in a variety
of styles to be produced easily.

A professional Web design program (which can cost hundreds of
pounds) saves a lot of work compared with typing HTML code.
However, it's a good idea to have at least a basic knowledge of writing
HTML code to support your use of the HTML editor.

Saving Your Work: .htm and .html

After you have created a Web page, by whatever method, it must be
saved (**File** and **Save As...**) with the file name extension **.htm** or **.html**.
You can use either extension but it's a good idea to consistently use
one or the other.

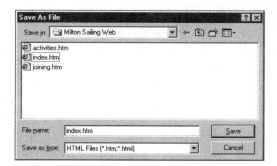

The Home Page: index.htm or index.html

Normally you would make up a meaningful name for the Web page such as **joining.htm**. The exception to this is the Home Page of any Web site, where it's the convention always to save it with the name **index.htm** or **index.html**. The use of this name causes all visitors to the site to be presented with the Home Page first.

Creating a New Folder for Your Web Files

A Web site may contain several pages saved as **.htm** or **.html** files, as well as other files, including graphics saved as **.gif** or **.jpeg** files. It's a good idea to collect all of the files for a particular Web site by placing them in a specially created folder of their own. The example below shows the folder for the fictitious Milton Sailing Club Web site, containing three Web pages and a graphic.

The new folder can be created in the **Windows Explorer** or **My Computer**. For example, suppose we wish to create a new folder as a sub-folder within the folder **Milton**. First highlight (using a single click) the folder **Milton** in the **Windows Explorer** or **My Computer**. Then select **File**, **New** and **Folder**. The **New Folder** icon appears in the highlighted folder. Replace **New Folder** with the name of your new Web site folder and press **Enter**.

You can also create a new folder when using the **Save As** dialogue box shown below. Click on the **Create New Folder** icon on the right-hand side then replace the words **New Folder** with a suitable name relevant to your own Web site.

The newly created folder can now be used for saving new Web pages. Any files needed for the new Web site which already exist in other folders can be moved into the new folder by dragging and dropping using **My Computer** or the **Windows Explorer**.

Viewing and Testing Web Pages

After you have entered and saved a Web page it should be opened for checking in your Web browser, such as Internet Explorer or Netscape Navigator. As you are likely to spend some time refining and developing the design before finally uploading it to the Internet, the browser should be set to work *off-line*, in order to avoid connection charges. Select **Work Offline** from the **Connect To** dialogue box, shown above, or **File** and **Work Offline** from the menu in Internet Explorer. In Netscape Navigator use **File** and **Offline**.

Apart from checking the spelling, you may wish to improve the layout and the choice of text and background colours. Links to other pages or Web sites should be tested. These can be corrected if necessary after returning to the text or HTML editor. Consider installing both Netscape Navigator and Internet Explorer on your computer, then you can check that your Web pages will be displayed correctly for the vast majority of Internet users.

Editing Web Pages

When building and editing a Web page it is often necessary to alternate between the text editor or the HTML editor and the finished Web page in the browser, such as Internet Explorer or Netscape Navigator. After viewing the finished page in the browser, you would return to the text or HTML editor to make any changes.

In **Netscape Navigator** selecting **File** and **Edit Page** launches the built-in **HTML** editor **Netscape Composer**.

After the Web page has been edited it should be saved again with the **.htm** or **.html** extension and checked in Internet Explorer, Netscape Navigator or whatever browser you are using.

Switching Between Programs

You may have several programs running simultaneously on your computer, although only one may be displayed on the screen, the rest running unseen in the background. For example, the Web browser may be on the screen, with the HTML editor or text editor running in the background. Programs currently running are each denoted by an icon on the Windows Taskbar at the bottom of the screen, as shown below.

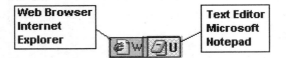

To display on the screen a program currently running in the background, simply click the Taskbar icon for the required program. The same method can be used to switch between an HTML editor and the Web browser or any other programs running on your computer.

Another way to alternate between running programs such as your Web browser and a text editor or an HTML editor is to continuously hold down the **Alt** key while making separate presses of the **Tab** key. This cycles through all of the programs currently running on your computer. Release the **Alt** key when the program you want is highlighted.

Publishing Your Web Pages

When you are happy with the pages you have created and saved on the **C:** drive of your own computer, they must be *uploaded* and saved on an Internet server computer. Then millions of people can (in theory) log on to the Internet and view your pages from anywhere in the world. When you subscribe to an Internet Service Provider (such as AOL) for your Internet connection, you may be allocated some free Web space (5-50MB perhaps) in which to save your work. Failing that, there are various organizations offering free Web space. In return, your Web site will automatically carry advertising banners for various products. Commercial organizations setting up a Web site may subscribe to a specialist Web hosting company. Services provided might include your own domain name e.g. **www.jimsmith.co.uk**, unlimited e-mail addresses and a counter to show how many people have visited your Web site.

Since the purpose of a Web site will be to promote products or communicate information to as wide an audience as possible, the next important task is to attract people to your site. This is done by placing key words within the Web pages and registering your pages with the various search engines which people use to surf the Internet.

The overall process for the creation of a Web site may be summarized as follows:

- Plan and design the layout of the individual Web pages and links to other pages, using pencil and paper

- Produce the HTML code using text editor, word processor or HTML editor/ Web design program.

- Save the HTML code as **.htm** or **.html** files

- Check the Web pages in one or more Internet browsers, such as Internet Explorer and Netscape Navigator.

- If necessary, return to the text or HTML editor and correct and modify the Web page as required.

- The finished Web pages should be saved along with any graphics images or other necessary files. These should all be placed in the same folder or directory.

- Arrange for a suitable domain name for your site and make arrangements with search engine providers to make your site accessible to as many people as possible.

- Upload the Web pages and any necessary graphics or other files to the Internet server of your Internet Service Provider or Web host, according to their instructions.

Summary:

That completes the overview of the process of creating a Web site. The following chapters look at the process in more detail. The next chapter covers the writing of your own HTML code. Some people may find the idea of writing HTML code to be too time-consuming and may well wish to miss the next chapter, moving straight on to the chapter **Creating Web Pages Using an HTML Editor**. However, if you can spend a few hours reading about HTML code, this will certainly be beneficial in the future.

Although you may create all your Web pages using an HTML editor like Microsoft FrontPage, Adobe Go Live or Macromedia DreamWeaver, it's generally agreed that some acquaintance with the principles of HTML is desirable. One reason for this is that it may sometimes be necessary to "tweak" the HTML code produced by the editor, in order to obtain a particular result which the HTML editor can't deliver.

Creating Web Pages by Writing HTML Code

Introduction

This chapter goes through the process of creating simple Web pages by writing the HTML code yourself (rather than using a software package such as an HTML editor to produce the code).

The work in this chapter is based on Notepad, a simple text editor provided as an **Accessory** with Microsoft Windows. Notepad creates simple *text files*, which use the standard ASCII format for text characters. This format is universally acceptable to computers in general. A small sample of HTML code produced in Notepad is shown below. You can see that it contains a lot of rather obscure commands (explained later) enclosed in angled brackets. In the example below, a command such as **<center>** is known as a *tag*. Tags are used to control the layout of the page. The text which is to appear on the Web page is enclosed between matching pairs of tags.

```
<html>
<head>
<title>Milton Rangers FC</title>
</head>
<body>
<h1><center>2001-2002 Season</center></h1>
<center><h7>Captain's Report</h7></center>
```

Please Note:

- Commands in tags may be entered in either upper or lower case letters, e.g. both **<title>** and **<TITLE>** are acceptable.

- The spellings **color** and **center** are used in HTML code.

After you have entered the HTML code into Notepad (or similar) it must be saved as a **Text Document** with the **.htm** or **.html** extension (either **.htm** or **.html** can be used as long as you consistently stick to one or the other.)

File name:	index.htm	▼	Save
Save as type:	Text Documents	▼	Cancel

Using a Word Processor to Type in HTML

You can also use a word processor like Microsoft Word or Corel WordPerfect to create HTML files, but care is needed as there can be problems. Type in the HTML code including tags and Web page content and, most importantly, save the work as a **Text Only** file, after selecting **File** and **Save As....** Save with either the **.htm** or **.html** extension.

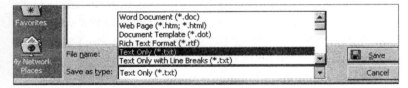

WARNING ! If you type HTML into a word processor such as Microsoft Word, do not use the option **Save as type: Web Page (*.htm,*.html)**. This method will not work since it is trying to translate instructions (which are already in HTML code) into HTML code.

(The option **Save as type: Web Page (*.htm,*.html)** is for converting an ordinary word processing document into HTML. This method is for people who don't want to type in HTML code.

The Structure of an HTML Page

All HTML pages have the same basic structure as shown below. The main feature of HTML code is the use of commands or *tags*, such as **<center>**, enclosed by angled brackets.

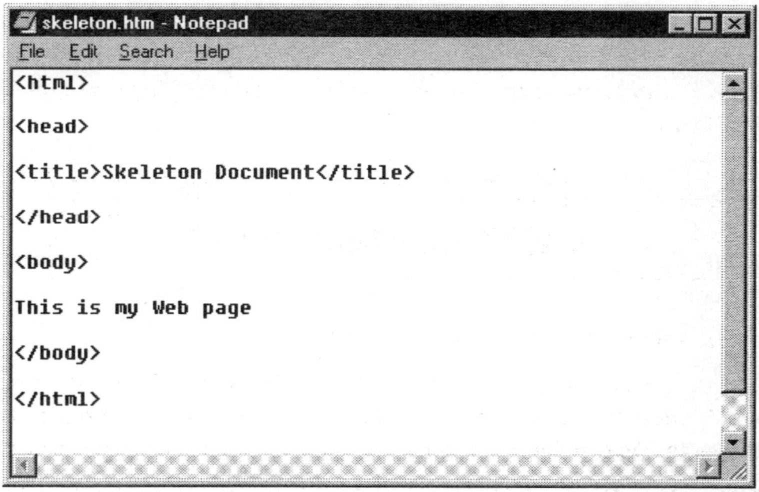

```
skeleton.htm - Notepad

File   Edit   Search   Help

<html>

<head>

<title>Skeleton Document</title>

</head>

<body>

This is my Web page

</body>

</html>
```

The entire Web page is enclosed by the brackets **<html>** and **</html>** denoting the fact that the document is an **.html** file. Note that for many, but not all, commands both an opening and a closing tag are used. The closing tag includes a forward slash, as in **</html>** above.

Text to be formatted is placed between opening and closing tags. For example, the word "Welcome" could be centred as shown below:

<center>Welcome</center>

Upper or Lower Case Commands

When typing in HTML commands, it doesn't matter whether you use upper case (i.e. capital) letters or lower case - or a mixture of both.

All Web pages consist of a *head* section and a *body* section, each defined by opening and closing tags, as shown above.

The head section includes a title, such as:

<title>Skeleton Document</title>

When the page is opened in a Web browser like Internet Explorer, the title, **Skeleton Document** in this example, appears in the title bar at the top left of the page, as shown below.

Referring to the previous skeleton Web page in HTML, after the head section is closed with **</head>**, the body section starts with **<body>**. The body section includes all of the text and graphics which are to appear on the Web page. The body section is closed with the **</body>** tag and the page is completed with the **</html>** closing tag.

Text Effects

Of course, a Web page will normally include far more content in the body section than shown in the previous skeleton Web page. You would normally insert both text and background colours, as well as graphic images and links to other pages.

HTML commands entered as tags are available to give most of the text effects normally applied in word processing and desktop publishing, such as different fonts, emphasizing text in bold and italic and layouts such as left and right aligned and centred.

These effects are normally switched on with an opening tag and switched off with a closing tag. For example, to embolden the text as in **Milton Garden Services** we would type:

<b>Milton Garden Services</b>

Similarly, to display the text in italics:

<i>Milton Garden Services</i>

Headings and Sub-headings

To specify the size of the letters in a heading, six tags are available, ranging from **<h1>** (largest) to **<h6>** (smallest). An indication of their size is as follows:

<h1>(large main heading)</h1>   (18pt)

<h3>(medium sub-heading)</h3> (14pt)

<h6>(small heading)</h6>   (10pt)

Please note that the tags **<h1>** through to **<h6>** don't simply alter the size of the letters. They also display the heading in bold text and insert two blank lines before and after the heading. So you don't need to insert the paragraph tags **<p>** and **</p>** (discussed shortly) and the embolden tags **** and **** when using the heading tags for titles and sub-headings.

Changing Background and Text Colours of the Entire Web Page

Common colours can be specified by typing in their names, such as **"red"**. You can specify the text colour and background colour for the entire Web page by placing commands within the opening **<body>** tag as shown in the following example:

```
<body bgcolor="cyan" text= "blue">

(Text and graphics content of the Web page)

</body>
```

It's important to choose a background colour which allows the text to be read easily - using the same colour for both text and background is obviously not a good idea.

Changing the Font Size, Colour and Typeface Locally

The tags **<font>** and **</font>** can be used to change the colour, size and typeface of the text in a particular part of the Web page. This method may be used to specify the appearance of just a single letter, word or paragraph of text, depending where you place the closing **</font>** tag. For example:

```
<font size="3" color="blue" face="arial">


(Text to be changed)


</font>
```

Note that the **font size** can vary between 1 and 7, with 7 being the largest. When specifying the typeface in the font tag, such as **face="arial"** above, you can get ideas by looking at the names of typefaces installed on your computer, such as Arial and Comic Sans MS for example. Select **Start**, **Settings**, **Control Panel** and double click the icon for the **Fonts** folder. To see what a particular font looks like, double click the icon for the font.

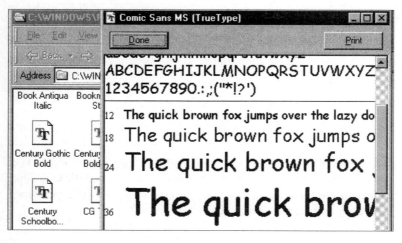

People visiting your Web site may not have the same fonts installed as those on your computer. It's therefore possible to specify more than one font in the **<font>** tag, separated by commas. For example,

<font size="3" color="blue" face="Arial", "Garamond">

In this example, if the first font, Arial, is not available on the visitor's computer, the second one listed, Garamond, will be substituted.

Choice of Colours for Text and Background
Colours Entered by Name

A choice of sixteen basic colours is available for the text and background of your Web page. These are specified by typing their name into the **<body>** tag e.g. **<body bgcolor="cyan" text= "blue">**. The text colour can also be specified as part of the **font** tag, for example **<font color= "cyan">**.

The sixteen colours entered by name are:

> **black, blue, cyan, gray, green, lime, magenta, maroon, navy, olive, purple, red, silver, teal, white, yellow**

Colours Entered by Hexadecimal Code

A much larger range of colours is available, each identified by a *hexadecimal code*. For example, **#c6eff7** is the code for light blue. The hexadecimal colour code is inserted in the opening **<body>** tag, to set the background colour of the whole document, for example:

<body bgcolor="#c6eff7">

To set the text colour for a single character, word, line or paragraph, a hexadecimal colour code can be inserted in the **<font>** tag as follows:

<font color="#b552ad">M</font>ilford

Note that the new colour is applied only to the text enclosed by the opening and closing font tags. So in the above example, the closing font tag **</font>** switches off the new font colour immediately after the **M** in Milford. The effect is to display only the letter **M** in the selected colour. Obtaining hexadecimal colour codes is quite complex and is discussed separately at the end of this section.

Page Layout Effects

Centring a Line or Paragraph

Opening and closing tags enclose the text to be centred.

(Text to be centred)

In the above tags, please note the American spelling, "center". The **<center>** and **</center>** tags need not only be applied to a single heading or line of text. They may be used to centre the whole of the body text, which may be several lines long.

```
<center>
(Text in body section)
</center>
```

Spacing and Line Breaks

When you are typing a document in HTML code into a text editor like Notepad, there's no point in using the space bar to put in extra spaces to improve the layout. Apart from single spaces between words, any additional spaces, carriage returns and line breaks are ignored when the HTML code is displayed as a Web page in a browser. Special commands for spacing, etc., are discussed below.

To check the layout of the finished Web page, save the file as an **.htm** or **.html** file in your text editor then load into the Web browser (such as Internet Explorer), working off-line.

The Paragraph Tag <p>

If you put **<p>** before a line of text, two blank lines are inserted before the paragraph. A further two blank lines are inserted if you use the **</p>** tag to close a paragraph. However, using multiple **<p>** tags does not increase the number of blank lines inserted - it's a one-off operation.

With some tags, such as the paragraph tag **<p>** above, the closing tag is not compulsory. (In this context a paragraph may be as little as a single word or line of text).

Inserting Single or Multiple Blank Lines

To insert *single* or *multiple* blank lines use the break tag **
**. The **
** tag (which is used without a closing tag) can also be used repeatedly to give any number of blank lines. For example, 3 blank lines would be given by **
**, **
**, **
**.

Inserting Spaces Within a Line of Text

Extra spaces between words (as produced by pressing the space bar when word processing) are inserted in a Web page by entering a *non-breaking space*, ** **, in the HTML code. This can be repeated for every space required, i.e. 3 spaces would be inserted by:

**   **

Aligning Text - Left, Right and Centre

The alignment attribute can be used to position various objects, including text. The align attribute can be included within a paragraph **<p>** (paragraph) tag as follows:

      <p align=left>(text to be aligned on the left)**</p>**

      <p align=right>(text to be aligned on the right)**</p>**

      <p align=center>(text to be aligned in the centre)**</p>**

Putting It All Together

The previous pages introduced some of the basic tags or commands used to control the layout of a Web page. There are many more tags, some of which are discussed later, such as those to insert graphics or to provide links between pages. However, the tags mentioned so far are enough to create a simple Web page, which can be saved and then checked in a Web browser such as Internet Explorer or Netscape Navigator.

It's a good idea to do a sketch plan of the page using pencil and paper, before typing the HTML code into a text editor like Microsoft Notepad.

Entering HTML Code into a Text Editor such as Notepad

Notepad is launched from **Start**, **Programs**, **Accessories** and **Notepad**. Notepad should open a new page automatically or you can select **File** and **New**. Start typing the HTML in, remembering that when the code is converted into a Web page all additional spaces (over and above single spaces between words) and carriage returns will be ignored. In the example which follows, lower case letters have been used for the commands in the tags. However, this is not compulsory and if you prefer you can use upper case or even a mixture of upper and lower case letters.

```
index.html - Notepad                                          _ 8 X
File  Edit  Search  Help
<html>

<head>
<title>Milton Home Page</title>
</head>

<body bgcolor="cyan"><font color="purple" face="comic sans MS">

<center><h1>Milton Garden Services</h1>

<h3>For All Your Gardening Needs</h3></center>

<p align=left><font size="2">
We are a small family business, established
since 1972. Why not call for a free estimate for any of your gardening
requirements, no matter how large or small.
</p></font>

<p align=center>Contact Milton Garden Services

<p align=center>View Our Range of Services

</font>
</body>
</html>
```

After you have typed the HTML code into Notepad it should be saved. (For a complex page it's obviously worth saving at regular intervals as the work progresses).

To save in Notepad, select **File** and **Save** or **Save As...**. You must select **Save as type: Text Documents** with the file name extension **.htm** or **.html** as shown in the following **Save As** dialogue box.

Creating a Separate Folder For All of Your Web Site's Files

When your Web site is complete it will consist of a lot of different files, including the Web pages themselves, plus any other files such as graphics or sound files. It's a good idea to create a new *folder* (also called a *directory*) just for the files for your Web site. This will also simplify the task of uploading the site to the Internet, when it's ready. There is an icon to create a new folder, on the top right of the **Save As** window shown above.

It's a good idea to give the folder a meaningful name, so that the files will be easier to find in the future. In this example I have created a new folder called **Milton Garden Services**. Once you have created a new folder, the files needed for your Web page can be moved into it by dragging and dropping in the Windows Explorer or in My Computer.

Saving the Home Page as index.htm or index.html

In this example, the page we have created is the Home Page of our Web site. It is the page which visitors to the site will see first. It's normal to save the home page with the file name **index.htm** or **index.html**. (Both **.htm** and **.html** are acceptable to modern systems). This has the effect of displaying the home page first whenever someone visits your Web site. Then they can use the *hyperlinks* (discussed shortly), to move to the other pages on your site).

Viewing a New Web Page

Having saved the HTML code produced in Notepad or another text editor, the newly created **.htm** or **.html** file can be opened in your Web browser such as Internet Explorer or Netscape Navigator.

For example, start up Internet Explorer from its icon on the desktop or from the menus using **Start**, **Programs** and **Internet Explorer**.

Set the browser to work *off-line* either in the **Connect To** dialogue box (as shown below) or in **File** and **Work Offline** from the Internet Explorer menu bar.

Connect To	? X
Connection to 0888181	
User name:	
Password:	
✓ Save password	
☐ Connect automatically	
Phone number:	0 845 0888181
Dialing from:	New Location ▼ Dial Properties...
Connect Properties Work Offline	

Next, from the Internet Explorer menu bar select **File** and **Open...** and **Browse** to find the required file, in this case **index.htm**.

In the window above, the **Open:** slot shows the path to the home page of our new web site.

C:\HTML\Milton Garden Services\index.htm

The hierarchy of folders/directories above is like the MS-DOS text-only operating system used before the arrival of graphical interfaces like Windows. **C:** is the hard disc drive and **HTML** is a folder (or directory) which I have created for storing Web sites. **Milton Garden Services** is the folder I created for storing all of the files for the Web site currently under construction. **index.htm** is the name of the home page for **Milton Garden Services**. After you click **OK** in the **Open** window shown above, the Web page opens in Internet Explorer.

If you are not happy with any aspect of the Web page you have just created, you need to return to the HTML code in Notepad (or whatever) to make the alterations. A quick way to return to the HTML code in Notepad is to click the Notepad icon on the Windows Taskbar at the bottom of the screen. When the HTML code has been modified it must be saved before being opened again for checking in your Internet browser. Continue alternating between correcting the HTML code in Notepad, saving the file and viewing the Web page off-line in the browser (Internet Explorer or Netscape Navigator). This process should continue until you are happy with the design of your Web page.

Exercise 3: Entering, Formatting and Saving Text

1. Start Notepad or an alternative text editor.

2. Copy the sample Web page shown on page 78. You may wish to change the content of the text to a subject of your own choice, while keeping all of the tags the same.

3. Create a new folder with a meaningful name, in which to save all of your Web pages.

4. Save the page as a text file with the name **index.htm** or **index.html**. This will be the Home Page of your Web site.

5. Start up your Web browser (e.g. Internet Explorer or Netscape Navigator) and set it to work *off-line*. Use **File** and **Open...** to view the Web page as it will appear on the Internet.

6. Check the Web page and note any changes to be made to the layout, appearance, or spelling.

7. Return to the HTML code in Notepad (or whatever). Use **View** and **Source**, etc., or click the icon on the Windows taskbar. Make any necessary alterations and repeat steps 4 onwards.

8. Use **File** and **Print** from the menus in your browser and text editor to make printouts on paper of:

    •   The finished Web page

    •   The HTML code

Adding Hyperlinks to Your Web Page

Hyperlinks are the parts of a Web page which you click to move to another page. A hyperlink normally consists of a piece of underlined blue text.

Return to Jim's Home Page

As you move the mouse cursor around the screen, it changes to a pointing hand whenever it passes over a hyperlink. A hyperlink can also take the form of a picture or graphic image. Large images can take a long time to load, causing frustration for the person surfing the Internet. By inserting a "thumbnail" or miniature version of the image on the Web page, the waiting time is reduced. The thumbnail image can be created as a hyperlink, linked to the full-size image. Anyone wishing to see the full version of the image simply clicks the thumbnail. Inserting pictures or images into a Web page is discussed shortly.

A hyperlink can be used (amongst other things) to:

- Move to another Web page in the current site
- Move to a new Web site
- Invite an e-mail

Moving to Another Web Page

The HTML code for a hyperlink takes the form:

< **a href**=" (destination Web page)">(Text to be clicked)</a>

Suppose we are on the Home Page of Milton Garden Services and we wish to view the details of the service offered by the company. A link **"View The Milton Service"** is placed in the hypertext as follows:

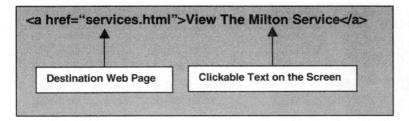

In the previous example, the destination Web page, **services.html,** was in the *same folder* as the currently selected Web page. If the destination is a Web page in a different folder, then the full *path name* would need to be given in the opening tag, for example:

< a href="horticulture/milton/services.html">

Links to Other Web Sites

To link to another Web site, the full Internet Address or URL (Uniform Resource Locator) is included in the opening tag, as follows:

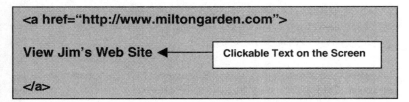

Inviting E-mail

A hyperlink can be used to make it easy for a visitor to send an e-mail directly to the provider of a Web page. For example, after reading a Web page about a new product or service, a visitor may wish to send an e-mail to the company, asking for further information. When the visitor clicks the hyperlink, this launches the e-mail program installed on their computer, with the company's e-mail address already infilled. The visitor simply types their message and clicks **Send**. The e-mail hyperlink is programmed by including **mailto:** and the e-mail address in the opening tag as shown below.

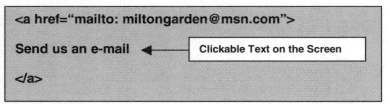

Please Note: Images can also act as clickable hyperlinks, as described later in this section in **"Using Thumbnails and Clickable Images"**.

Working with Pictures

A Web page will often need to be illustrated by the addition of pictures or graphic images. These may take the form of photographs, ready-made drawings (or *clip-art*), or graphics you have produced yourself using a drawing or paint program. Whatever the source of the pictures, you need to guard against over-zealous use of images. This is because images can be very bulky, making them slow to download from the Internet server to the user's computer. The effect of this is to cause frustration to the person browsing the Web as they wait for your pages to load. Obviously it pays therefore to include only those images which are really essential to support the text. There are several steps (discussed in detail later) which can help with the loading of graphics:

- Save the file in a compressed format.

- Specify the dimensions of the graphic (height and width) in the HTML code which inserts the image.

- Keep the dimensions of the image small, possibly with a link to a full-size image. A miniature version of an image, known as a *thumbnail*, is often used.

- Provide some relevant "alternate" text which appears in place of the graphic until it has downloaded from the Internet.

Image Formats

There are several formats for saving graphics images as files. These are distinguished by the file name extensions such as **.bmp**, **.jpeg** or **.gif**. The extensions are selected from **Save as type:** and added to the file name when you save a file in a graphics program such as Windows Paint or Paint Shop Pro. In the example below, the file might be saved as **daff.gif** or **daff.jpeg**.

File name:	daff.gif	▼	Save
Save as type:	Graphics Interchange Format (*.gif)	▼	Cancel
	Monochrome Bitmap (*.bmp;*.dib)		
	16 Color Bitmap (*.bmp;*.dib)		
	256 Color Bitmap (*.bmp;*.dib)		
	24-bit Bitmap (*.bmp;*.dib)		
	JPEG File Interchange Format (*.jpg;*.jpeg)		
	Graphics Interchange Format (*.gif)		

Graphics File Name Extensions

Among the most common graphics file formats and their extensions are:

Windows Bitmap: Extension .bmp

Windows' own format, used by default when a graphic is saved in a Windows program such as Paint. The bitmap gives good quality but as there is no compression, the bitmap takes up too much space for efficient use in Web pages.

Joint Photographic Experts Group: Extension .jpeg

This is a compressed format especially suitable for storing photographs economically for use in Web pages or for sending with e-mails.

Compuserve Graphics Interchange Format: Extension .gif

This format combines relatively small size with good quality images. The **.gif** format is the most popular for images used in Web pages.

Saving Files as .gifs or .jpegs

Drawings in the Windows Paint program can be saved as **.gif** or **.jpeg** files. Image editing software like Paint Shop Pro and Adobe PhotoShop have facilities for compressing and manipulating images prior to use on the Internet. A time-limited evaluation version of Paint Shop Pro (shown below) can be obtained from:

http:// www.jasc.com

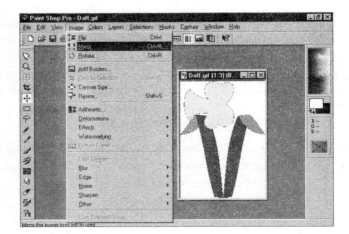

Inserting a Graphic into a Web Page

As stated earlier, it's convenient if all of the files connected with a Web site are stored in the same folder. In this example, based on Milton Garden Services, so far we have a home page **index.html** saved in the folder Milton Garden Services. We can also add the picture of a flower **daff.gif**, by dragging and dropping from its previous location, using the Windows Explorer or My Computer. The contents of the new Web site folder would now be as follows:

To include the picture **daff.gif** in the Web page, the following line would be inserted in the HTML code:

<img src="daff.gif">

When inserting graphics all of the information is included within the **<img>** tag. There must always be a statement **src="**(location of graphic)**"** where the location is the path to the graphic file. For example, if the graphic was in a sub-folder called **pictures**, the instruction would become:

<img src="pictures/daff.gif">

Please note that the forward slash "/" is used in path names to files when writing HTML code as shown above. This contrasts with the back slash "\" used in Windows and the earlier MS-DOS operating system, e.g.   **C:\HTML\Milton Garden Services\daff.gif**

A number of other attributes can be specified within the **<img>**tag:

Alternate Text: The alt Attribute

For example, **alt="picture of a daffodil"** would cause the text in speech marks to appear in advance of the picture, while the picture is being downloaded. The alternate text will also appear later, if you allow the cursor to hover over the picture.

height and width

If you specify these dimensions in the **<img>**, the image will load more quickly. These measurements are stated in pixels, i.e. the small picture elements which make up an image on the screen. A typical screen resolution is 640 x 480 pixels. You can find the size of an image in Paint Shop Pro, for example, by selecting **View** and **Image Information** as follows:

```
Current Image Information                                    [X]

| Image Information | Creator Information |

  ┌─ Source File ──────────────────────────────────────────────┐
  │ File Name:              c:\Html\Milton Garden Services\daff.gif │
  │ File Type:                              CompuServe GIF        │
  └────────────────────────────────────────────────────────────┘

  ┌─ Image ──────────────────┐  ┌─ Status ─────────────────────┐
  │ Dimensions:  262 x 370 Pixels │  │ Has Been Modified:      Yes │
  │              3.64 x 5.14 Inches│  │ Has a Selection:         No │
  │ Pixels Per Inch:          72 │  │ Number of Layers:         1 │
  │ Pixel Depth/Colors:    8/256 │  │ Number of Alphas:         0 │
```

The **Dimensions:** note above shows that the **daff.gif** image has a width of 262 pixels and a height of 370 pixels. The attributes **height=370 width=262** would be included in the **<img>** tag as shown in the next example. The **align** attribute can be used to position the image against the left and right margins and also to align the top, middle or bottom of the image with the text on the line. An image is centred by enclosing the **<img>** tag within the tags **<center>** and **</center>**.

<img src="daff.gif"alt="picture of a daffodil" height=370 width=262 align=left>

The **<img>** tag also has attributes for including a border and vertical and horizontal space around an image, stated in pixels. For example:

border=10   vspace=20   hspace=40

These can be placed within the **<img>** tag as follows:

<img src="daff.gif"alt="picture of a daffodil" height=370 width=262 align=left border=10 vspace=20 hspace =40>

Please Note: Images can also act as clickable hyperlinks, as described later in this section in **"Using Thumbnails and Clickable Images"**.

The next exercise gives practice in the ideas covered so far. You may wish to copy the HTML code exactly as given. Alternatively you may wish to alter the content to a topic of your own choice, while keeping the tags and commands the same.

Before starting the exercise, make sure you have done the following:

1. Completed the exercise on page 82 and saved the file with the name **index.htm** or **index.html**.

2. Created a new folder such as **Milton Garden Services** in which you have saved a copy of **index.htm** or **index.html**.

3. Created or obtained a graphic image and saved it as a **.gif** file in your new Web site folder, using Microsoft Paint or Paint Shop Pro, as previously described.

If you are copying the text for Milton Garden Services, your Web site folder will be something like:

Exercise 4: Inserting Hyperlinks and Graphics

1. Start Notepad or whatever program you are using as a text editor.

2. Copy the following HTML code:

```
services.html - Notepad                                        _ 8 X
File  Edit  Search  Help

<html>
<head>
<title>Milton Service</title>
</head>
<body bgcolor="lime"><font color="navy" face="comic sans MS">
<center><h1>The Milton Service</h1></center>
<center><img src="daff.gif"alt="picture of a daffodil" height=94
width=65 border=5></center>
<h3>Our Staff</h3>
<font size="2">We are fortunate in having a very experienced staff
capable of undertaking a wide range of gardening work. All types
of job undertaken, from regular garden maintenance to large
landscaping projects.
<h3>Services include:</h3>
<center>Garden Design and consultancy
<br>Landscaping and planting
<br>Construction of paths, ponds and patios
<br>Lawn mowing, hedge cutting and weed control</center>
<p><center><a href="index.html">Back to Home Page</a></center>
</font>
</body>
</html>
```

3. After you have finished typing the HTML, carefully check for spelling mistakes and correct if necessary.

4. Save the Web page with the name **services.html** (or **.htm**) in the Web site folder **Milton Garden Services**.

5. Now load the new file using **File** and **Open...** into your Web browser such as Internet Explorer or Netscape Navigator, working off-line.

6. You may need to select **Browse...** to locate the folder you created for saving your Web pages. When you select **Open** and click **OK** the new Web page should open as shown on the next page.

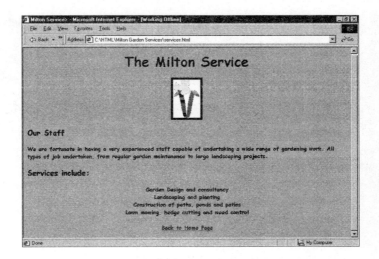

7.   Test the link back to the Home Page by clicking on **Back to Home Page**. If the link doesn't work correctly, make sure the tag **<a href="index.html">** is exactly right as shown in the code in step **2.** on the previous page. If you are not happy with any aspect of the Web page, return to the HTML code in the text editor (Notepad, etc.) and make the improvements. For example, you could change the background colour **bgcolor** in the **<body>** tag, or the text colour (**color**) in the **<font>** tag.

8.   Save the HTML code and check the Web page again in your browser. Repeat the process of checking and editing until you are happy with the Web page.

9.   Now load the HTML code for your Home Page into your text editor (Notepad, etc.) It was recommended that the Home Page was saved with the name **index.htm** or **index.html**. At the bottom of the page insert a link from the Home Page to the **services.htm** or **services.html** page.

The new link should be something like:

   <a href="services.html">View Our Range of Services</a>

10. Save this modified version of **index.html**, load it into your Web browser (Internet Explorer, Netscape Navigator, etc.) and check that the new link works correctly.

11. With the HTML code for the new version of **index.html** open in your text editor, insert the graphic which you should have obtained (as described on page 89.)

12. Save the code and then load **index.html** into your Web browser to check the layout of the page. If necessary, return to the text editor and modify the HTML code if necessary.

13. Use **File** and **Print** from the menus in your browser and text editor to make printouts on paper of:

• The two finished Web pages **index.html** and **services.html**.

• The HTML code for both pages.

At this stage, you should now have two complete Web pages, **index.html** and **services.html**, which include links connecting the pages in both directions. The Web site folder now contains the files for the two Web pages plus the graphic **daff.gif**.

Exercise 5: Writing Your Own HTML Code

In the next exercise you are only given the text which is to appear on the screen for the third Web page.

1. Use your text editor to enter the following, together with the HTML code to create the document as a Web page.

Milton Garden Services

How to Contact Us

E-mail
Garden design and landscaping: marybrown@milton.co.uk
Hard landscaping and building: davidwalker@milton.co.uk
Garden maintenance: edwinsmith@milton.co.uk

Or contact us by telephone or in person at:
Milton Garden Services
Elm Tree Cottage
Oakwell

OE7 9XZ

Tel. 01754 49832

Return to Home Page

---

2. Format the text **Milton Garden Services** as a Heading in the large font size.

    Format the text **How to Contact Us** as a Subheading in the medium font size.

    Format the remainder of the text as Body Text in the small font size.

    Include clear line spacing as shown above.

3. Centre the title **Milton Garden Services**, the address details and the link **Return to Home Page**. All other text to be left-aligned on the page.

    Embolden the telephone number

    Italicise the text **Or contact us by telephone or in person at:**

4. Import the graphic **daff.gif** and position it below the text Milton Garden Services and above the text **How to Contact Us**. Ensure that the graphic is centre-aligned on the page.

5. The new page should link back to the Milton Garden Service Home Page. Edit the new page to link the text **Return to Home Page** to the **index.html** page.

    Save the new page to disc with a name like **contact.html**.

6. The Home Page must be linked to the new page. Load the page **index.html** into your text editor and locate the text:

    Contact Milton Garden Services

    Edit this text to be a link to the new page, **contact.html**.

7. Load all three pages into the browser and test all of the links.

8. Change the background colour of the **index.html** Home Page ensuring that it is different from the text colour.

    Save the amended **index.html** page.

9. Edit the new page **contact.html** so that each of the three e-mail addresses shown below are "live" e-mail links:

    marybrown@milton.co.uk

    davidwalker@milton.co.uk

    edwinsmith@milton.co.uk

    Save the amended **contact.html** page to disc.

10. Load each of the pages **index.html**, **services.html** and **contact.html** into the browser and print a copy a copy of each.

    Print a copy of the HTML code for each of the 3 pages.

11. Exit from the applications following the correct procedures.

The 3 pages for your Web site should now be complete. You can always edit them to include latest information, improve the layout, colours and design or to correct any spelling mistakes. The Web site folder should now contain files for each of the 3 Web pages, plus the graphic **daff.gif**.

Reminder: .htm or .html

You can save your Web pages with either of the file name extensions **.htm** or **.html**. Early versions of Windows could only handle **.htm**. The only requirement is that you are consistent. For example, if your Home Page is named **index.htm** and you tried to open it by typing **index.html** you will get a **File not found** message.

Using Thumbnails and Clickable Images

Large images occupy a lot of disc space and memory, making Web pages very slow to download completely and causing frustration to Internet surfers. To make a Web page download more quickly, you can initially load a miniature version of a graphic, known as a "thumbnail". Once the page has downloaded, anyone wishing to view the full picture can do so by clicking on the thumbnail. Programs like Microsoft Paint and Paint Shop Pro can be used to resize the image down to a thumbnail and also provide the numbers for the new **height** and **width** in pixels, to be used in the **<img>** tag which loads the graphic image.

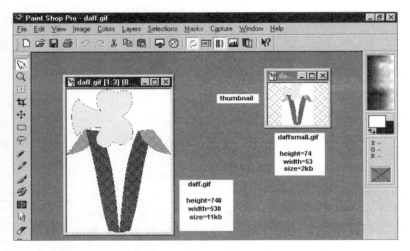

It's better to save a scaled down version of an image for use as a thumbnail. The alternative (slower) method would be to create the thumbnail by loading the full-size image file from disc, scaling down with reduced **height** and **width** attributes in the **<img>** tag.

In this example, a thumbnail version of the daffodil is saved in the Web site folder as a separate file, **daffsmall.gif**, as shown above in Paint Shop Pro. This will be loaded into the Home Page, **index.html**, specifying suitable small dimensions for **height** and **width**.

<img src="daffsmall.gif" height=74 width=53 >

Making an Image into a Hyperlink

The general form to make a graphic into a "clickable" hyperlink is:

```
<a href ="(Destination Web Page, etc.)">
<img src="(Name of clickable image)">
</a>
```

Please note that the destination can be a file, such as the full-size image **daff.gif** accessed from the thumbnail **daffsmall.gif**.

To modify the main Web page **index.html** to include the clickable thumbnail image, we can add the following HTML code.

```
<center>
<a href="daff.gif">
<img src="daffsmall.gif"height=74 width=53>
</a>
</center>
```

(For simplicity in this example, the attributes for spacing, alternate text and border have been omitted from the **<img>** tag.)

Please note in this example, the coding is simplified because images such as **daff.gif** are in the same folder as the Web pages like **index.html**, as shown below. If not, you would have to refer to them by their full path name, for example: **Images/Gardening/daff.gif**

After saving the new version of **index.html**, the Home Page opens up in the browser with the thumbnail image displayed. Clicking on the thumbnail invokes the full-size image in its own window. If you wish to return to the Home Page from the full-size image you need to click **Back** on the browser.

Obtaining Hexadecimal Colour Codes

If you want to use colours other than the sixteen well-known colours which can be specified by their name, you need to know the hexadecimal code for the colour, as discussed earlier. These codes are entered in the **<body>** tag or the **<font>** tag, for example:

<body bgcolor="#c6eff7">

<font color="#b552ad">Milford</font>

The hexadecimal system is based on the number sixteen and has the "digits" 0 1 2 3 4 5 6 7 8 9 a b c d e f. Every colour has 3 components, Red, Green and Blue, each represented by a number, as shown in the following extract from the **Edit Colors** feature in Microsoft Paint.

The component numbers for Red, Green, Blue for the selected colour are 128, 64 and 64 in decimal. Converting these to hexadecimal gives the codes 80, 40, 40. The selected colour would therefore be written in HTML code as **#804040** and used in the **<body>** and **<font>** tags as previously described e.g. **<body bgcolor="#804040">**.

If you have a copy of Paint Shop Pro, the hexadecimal colour codes for use in HTML coding are calculated for you in the **Edit Palette** feature.

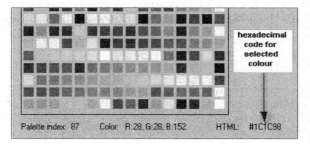

hexadecimal
code for
selected
colour

Palette index: 87   Color: R:28, G:28, B:152   HTML: #1C1C98

Publishing Your Web Site

At this stage you should have a separate folder containing all of the Web pages and the graphics file necessary for the simple Web site created in the previous exercises.

The next stage is to upload the files to the server of the Internet Service Provider who will host your site. Precise instructions for this task are provided by individual ISPs, but the subject is discussed in more detail in the final chapter of this book, **Publishing Your Web Site**.

Checking Your Progress

The next page gives a list of the basic skills needed for creating Web pages, as covered in this chapter. The same skills are included in the next chapter, which describes the creation of Web pages using HTML editing (i.e. Web design) software, such as Microsoft FrontPage. For convenience, since readers may wish to assess their progress using both methods, the skills list is repeated at the end of the next chapter.

Checklist of Basic Internet Skills

This list follows closely the Assessment Objectives of Element 3: Publish Information on a Web Site, of the Internet Technologies Stage 1 course from Oxford Cambridge and RSA Examinations. You might wish to check your progress against this list and, if necessary, revisit any topics requiring further work.

Objective	Achieved
Insert an image into a document, align and resize.	☐
Use 3 different font sizes, small, medium, large.	☐
Embolden specified text.	☐
Italicise specified text.	☐
Align page items as specified - left, right, centre.	☐
Change the background colour of a document.	☐
Link existing pages via specified text.	☐
Link new page to existing pages via specified text.	☐
Link existing pages to new page via specified text.	☐
Link specified text to a specified e-mail address.	☐
Link specified text to a specified URL (http://)	☐
Store the Web pages to disc.	☐
Print Web pages from the browser software.	☐
Print HTML source code for all Web pages.	☐
Exit the software using the correct procedure.	☐

Creating Web Pages Using an HTML Editor

Introduction

The last section covered the writing of HTML code by typing the commands or tags into a simple text editor like Microsoft Notepad. A knowledge of HTML is helpful in understanding the construction of Web pages but coding by hand is very time-consuming and exacting. Not surprisingly, therefore, a large number of software packages have been developed to simplify the task of creating Web pages. These are known as HTML editors and allow you to create Web pages without having to type in the actual HTML commands. In fact, the task is very similar to word processing. You simply enter the text, insert any graphical images and the editor creates all of the HTML commands for you. When using an HTML editor, it's still possible to view the HTML code and, if necessary, edit it manually in a text editor like Notepad. Internet Explorer includes its own HTML editor, FrontPage Express, launched form **Start**, **Programs** and **Internet Explorer**.

FrontPage Express is a basic HTML editor which will allow you to follow the work in this section, while FrontPage 2000 is a more powerful professional version which can be purchased separately. Anyone familiar with Microsoft Word will immediately feel at home with Microsoft FrontPage as the two programs have very similar "user interfaces".

Macromedia DreamWeaver is another Web design program which is very popular with professionals. Programs like these enable Web pages to incorporate powerful features such as animations, music, video clips, menus, buttons, forms and tables.

Creating a Home Page

As FrontPage Express is readily available on most PCs, it will be referred to frequently in this section, which is based on the fictitious Milton Sailing Club. First we will complete a simple Home Page, something like the one below, opened in Internet Explorer.

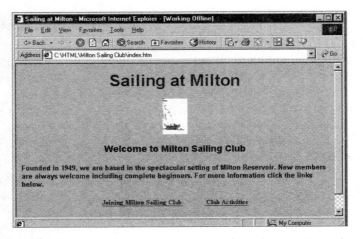

Entering the Text

FrontPage Express is launched after selecting **Start**, **Programs** and **Internet Explorer**. Start entering the text as if you are using a word processor.

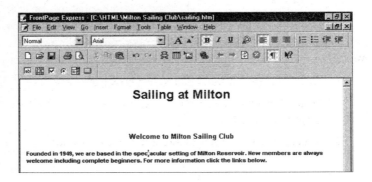

Text Effects

All of the common word processing text effects are available on the FrontPage Express Format Toolbar across the top of the screen. For readers not familiar with word processing, the meanings of the most frequently used icons are given on the diagram below.

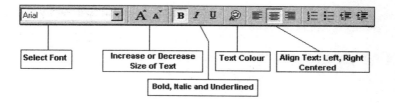

| Select Font | Increase or Decrease Size of Text | Text Colour | Align Text: Left, Right Centered |

Bold, Italic and Underlined

These effects can be applied in either of two ways:

Method 1:

1. Type all of the text first, in the default font, e.g., Times New Roman.

2. Select, i.e. highlight, the relevant text using the mouse.

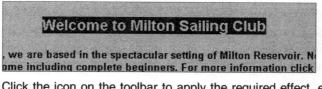

3. Click the icon on the toolbar to apply the required effect, e.g. **bold** or *italic* text.

4. Click outside of the text to remove the highlighting.

Method 2

1. Click the icon for the required text effect, to switch it on.

2. Enter the text, which should appear with the effect already applied as you type.

3. Click the icon for the text effect to switch it off again.

Changing Font

A font or style of lettering is selected after clicking on the down arrow to the right of the default font name, normally Times New Roman. If you choose a very unusual font, it may not be available to visitors to your Web site, depending on what fonts have been installed on their computer.

Changing Font Size

Select the required piece of text. When using FrontPage Express, click either of the icons shown left to increase or decrease the font size.

More precise control over font size (amongst other things) is given by selecting **Format** and **Font...** from the menu bar. This shows the more usual method of specifying font sizes, i.e. using *points*, where 72 pt represents letters one inch high.

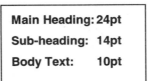

Typical font sizes in a Web page might be, for example:

> **Main Heading:** 24pt
>
> **Sub-heading:** 14pt
>
> **Body Text:** 10pt

Bold and Italic Text

These two effects are applied to selected text by clicking
the icons on the toolbar.

The effects can also be switched on before typing the required text and
switched off afterwards. Effects like these act as "toggles" - they are
switched on and off in the same way, i.e. by clicking the icon.

Text Alignment

Selected text can be aligned either left, centred or right,
as indicated by the alignment icons on the toolbar
shown on the right. The paragraph below has been selected and then
left aligned.

Founded in 1949, we are based in the spectacular setting of Milton Reservoir. New members
are always welcome including complete beginners. For more information click the links
below.

Text can also be aligned using **Format** and **Paragraph...** from the
menu bar.

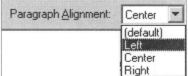

In this context, a paragraph can mean a single word used in a heading,
for example, as well as a more typical paragraph consisting of several
sentences.

Selecting Text

Text is selected, i.e. highlighted against a dark background, by dragging
the cursor over it. (Or hold down the shift key and press one of the four
arrow keys as required.)

Text Colour

FrontPage Express has several ways to change the colour of selected text. The easiest method is probably to click the **Text Color** icon on the toolbar, as shown left. This brings up a grid of available basic colours, together with a feature for adding user-defined or **Custom Colors**.

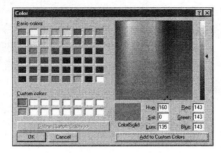

The text colour can also be changed using **Format** and **Font...** and **Format** and **Background...** (discussed below).

Background Colour

The background colour of the whole page can be changed by selecting **Format** and **Background...** then clicking the down arrow to the right of the **Background:** slot. It is necessary to keep the mouse button pressed down while moving over the choice of colours, before releasing the button over the chosen colour. This feature also allows the colour of **Text:** to be changed for the whole document. (This does not override the colours of individual pieces of text where the colours have been set separately.)

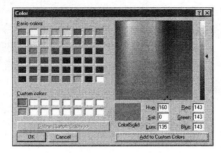

Saving a Web Page

This section has so far looked at entering the text for a Web page and applying various effects. Later pages cover the insertion of pictures and the use of hyperlinks to enable visitors to move to different pages. Next, however, the important topic of saving a Web page is covered. First select **File** and **Save As...** then click the **As File...** button, to open the **Save As File** dialogue box shown below.

Saving as index.htm or (index.html)

When saving a Home Page it is normal to use the name **index.htm** or **index.html**. The use of the name **index** ensures that this page will be seen first by visitors to the site. The file name extensions **.htm** and **.html** are both acceptable, but FrontPage Express uses **.htm** by default. Make sure the **Save as type:** slot is set to **HTML Files(*.htm,.html)**.

Creating a New Folder

It's very convenient if all of the files (Web pages, graphics, etc.) relating to a Web site are stored in their own separate folder (also known as a directory). It's easy to create this new folder while saving the page in the **Save As File** dialogue box shown above. Clicking on the **Create New Folder** icon allows you to replace the words **New Folder** with a meaningful name for your site. In the above example, the folder **Milton Sailing Club** had been created earlier.

Viewing a Web Page in a Browser

Having created and saved the text for a Web page, you need to check that it will be displayed correctly in the popular Web browsers, namely Internet Explorer and Netscape Navigator. In the Netscape Navigator browser use **File** and **Open Page** and **Choose File....** (Viewing a Web page using the Internet Explorer browser is discussed on pages 124 and 125.)

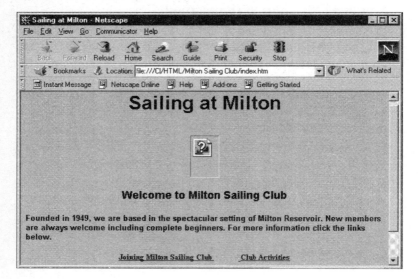

While the Web pages are under development, with all necessary files stored on your local hard disc, it makes sense to set your browser to work *off-line*, i.e. not connected to the Internet

After you click **Open** the Web page should be displayed as it will be seen on the Internet.

Editing a Web Page

Having viewed a new Web page in a browser such as Internet Explorer or Netscape Navigator, you can return to the HTML editor such as FrontPage to carry out any modifications. This might include changes to the size and colour of the text or corrections to the spelling, for example. Internet Explorer makes it easy to return to FrontPage by including the option **Edit with Microsoft FrontPage** accessed off the **File** menu. Alternatively you can have both the browser and the HTML editor running at the same time and switch between them by clicking their icons on the Windows Taskbar at the bottom of the screen.

Netscape Navigator has a built-in HTML editor, Netscape Composer. With a Web page open for viewing in Navigator, click **File** and **Edit Page** to launch the editor, **Netscape Composer**, as shown below.

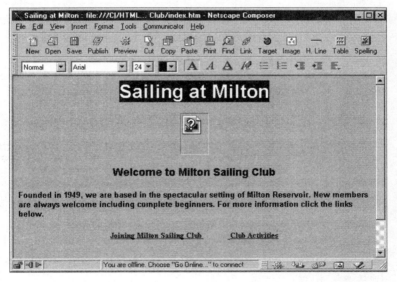

After making any changes to the Web page in the HTML editor, the page should again be saved and viewed in the browser, Netscape Navigator or Internet Explorer. This process of editing and saving may need to be repeated until you are satisfied with the content and appearance of the Web page.

Viewing the HTML Code

An HTML editor like FrontPage or DreamWeaver takes much of the hard work out of producing Web pages, by generating the actual HTML code which controls the page layout. However, there may be occasions when you need to examine the code, perhaps to make some fine tuning adjustments which are proving difficult using the editor software.

With a Web page open in Internet Explorer, you can display the HTML code for the page by selecting **View** and **Source**. This causes the Notepad program to open, displaying the HTML code, which can then be edited. (An introduction to HTML coding is given in the previous chapter, Creating Web Pages By Writing HTML Code).

In Netscape Navigator you can view the HTML code of a Web page by selecting **View** and **Page Source**.

To view the HTML code for a page open in Microsoft FrontPage, click the **HTML** tab at the bottom of the screen.

```
<p align="left"><font size="2">This Web site is maintained by:
Jim Gatenby</font></p>

<p> </p>
</body>
```

Working with Images

A Web page will often need to be illustrated with pictures or photographs. Most Internet graphics are saved in the Compuserve Graphics Interchange Format with the (**.gif**) file name extension. Photographic images normally use the Joint Photographic Experts Group (**.jpeg** or **.jpg**) format, as discussed on page 86. For general Internet use therefore, any graphics to be imported into a Web page should be converted into **.gif** files. Images in other formats such as **.bmp** can be loaded into a program like Microsoft Paint (**Start, Programs, Accessories, Paint**) and resaved in the **.gif** format.

File name:	yacht.gif		Save
Save as type:	Graphics Interchange Format (*.gif)		Cancel

Monochrome Bitmap (*.bmp;*.dib)
16 Color Bitmap (*.bmp;*.dib)
256 Color Bitmap (*.bmp;*.dib)
24-bit Bitmap (*.bmp;*.dib)
JPEG File Interchange Format (*.jpg;*.jpeg)
Graphics Interchange Format (*.gif)

opics on the Help M

The popular Paint Shop Pro software is a reasonably priced image editing tool and very useful for this sort of work. A trial version is available at: **http://www.jasc.com**

As stated previously, it's a good idea to create a new folder to hold all of the files for a Web site. This will include all of the Web pages and any graphics files. So, for example, the Milton Sailing Club folder might have 3 pages, **index.htm**, **activities.htm**, **joining.htm** and the graphic **yacht.gif**.

Gathering all of the files for a Web site into a single folder makes it simpler to load any graphics and also to publish the Web site on the Internet.

Sources of Graphic Images

The graphics you import onto your Web pages may be, for example:

- Drawings you have created yourself and saved as **.gifs** in a drawing or painting program.

- Photographs stored in the **.jpeg** or **.jpg** formats.

- Ready-made clip art images available on your hard disc, CD or from the Internet.

Inserting a Graphic Image

The basic method in FrontPage Express is:

1. Place the cursor at the insertion point for the picture.

2. Select from the menus **Insert**, **Image**, **From File** and **Browse....**

3. Locate the required graphic and click **Open** to insert the image on the page.

Adjusting the Size of a Graphic Image

If you click anywhere over a graphic, 8 small squares appear around the outside, as shown below. This indicates that the graphic has been selected. To resize the image, drag one of the small squares in one of the corners until the image is the required size.

Aligning a Graphic Image

The image can be aligned by highlighting it then selecting align left, right or centre from the **Formatting** bar, as shown below.

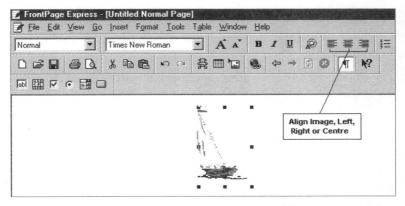

Scaling Down Graphic Images for Faster Downloading

Large pictures generally have a large file size on disc, making Web pages slow to download from the Internet. This waiting is likely to cause the visitor to your Web site to lose interest. It's a good idea to reduce the size of an image by scaling it down in a program like Microsoft Paint. An image can be reduced by "stretching it" by less than 100% in the horizontal and vertical directions. (Select **Image** and **Stretch/Skew...**).

Then the reduced size image should be saved (as a separate **.gif** file) before being inserted into the Web page in FrontPage, etc.

Thumbnail Images

Sometimes a very small image (known as a **thumbnail**) is loaded initially. A visitor who really wants to see the full size image can do so by clicking the thumbnail, which is linked to the full size image. This is discussed further in the next section

You can check the effect of any scaling down in Microsoft Paint by selecting **Image** and **Attributes....**

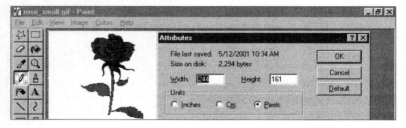

Width: and **Height:** in this example are given in *pixels* or picture elements. Pixels are small rectangles which make up the screen. Screens can be set at typical resolutions of 640x480, 800x600 or 1024x768 pixels - the higher the number of pixels, the sharper the image. So, in the above example, if the resolution was set at 640x480, the image of 244x161 pixels would occupy (very roughly) a third of the *total* screen height and a third of the *total* screen width.

Alternate Text

This is text which appears on the screen at the location of a graphic image. This avoids an empty space if there is delay while the image is being downloaded. Alternate text also appears if you allow the cursor to hover over an image displayed on a Web page. You could, for example, add a note such as **Click here to see full size picture**, to appear over a thumbnail image linked to a full size picture.

The FrontPage HTML editor allows you to add alternate text after right-clicking over the image and selecting **Picture Properties....**

The **Low-Res:** slot above allows you to specify a low resolution version of a graphic, which will load very quickly into a browser to occupy the empty space on the screen while the high resolution version is being downloaded. The low resolution version must have been prepared and saved earlier in a location which can be selected after clicking **Browse...** as shown above.

Preparing for Exercise 6

The next exercise covers all of the skills covered so far in this chapter. Before starting work you need a graphic image relevant to a Web page about sailing. This might be a piece of clip art or a simple picture drawn in Paint or similar program. Adjust the size of the image if necessary. Save the image as a **.gif** file, with a suitable name such as **yacht.gif**. You might also create a new folder, **Milton Sailing Club**, in Windows Explorer or My Computer. This can be used to store all of the Web pages plus the prepared image **yacht.gif**.

Exercise 6: Editing, Formatting and Saving a Web Page

1. Start up your HTML editor program with a new Web page open.

2. Enter the following text:

> Sailing at Milton
>
> Welcome to Milton Sailing Club
>
> Founded in 1949, we are based in the spectacular setting of Milton Reservoir. New members are always welcome including complete beginners. For more information click the links below.
>
> Joining Milton Sailing Club
>
> Club Activities
>
> This Web site is maintained by:

3. Enter your name after: **This Web is site maintained by:**

    Format the text **Sailing at Milton** as a Heading in the large font size.

    Format the text **Welcome to Milton Sailing Club** as a Subheading in the medium font size.

    Format all other text as Body Text in the small font size.

    Ensure that each of the 6 paragraphs is separated by a clear linespace.

4. Format the paragraph starting **Founded in 1949...** and the last paragraph **This Web is site maintained by:** to be left aligned on the page. Format all other paragraphs to be centre-aligned on the page.

    Embolden the text **including complete beginners**.

    Italicise the text **Welcome to Milton Sailing Club**.

The page must include the yacht graphic which you have previously prepared.

5. Import the graphic **yacht.gif** and position it below the text **Sailing at Milton** and above the text **Welcome to Milton Sailing Club**. Ensure that the graphic is centre-aligned on the page. Adjust the size of the graphic, if necessary.

6. Save the new page on disc with the name **index.htm**.

7. Load the new page into the Web browser and check the appearance and spelling.

8. Return to the HTML editor and correct any mistakes. Change the background and text colours.

9. Save the amended **index.htm** page to disc.

10. Print a copy of the Web page from your browser.

11. Print a copy of the HTML code for the Web page.

Adding Hyperlinks to Your Web Page

In the previous exercise there were two lines of text which were to be typed in but (at that stage) served no useful purpose. These were:

Joining Milton Sailing Club

Club Activities

The intention is that each of these lines of text can be clicked, leading to a new page, giving further information. These lines of "clickable" text are known as **hyperlinks** and are fundamental to the Internet.

Hyperlinks normally appear in underlined blue text. As described later, a graphic image can also act as a hyperlink. The cursor changes to a pointing hand when you hover over a piece of text or a graphic which has been converted to a hyperlink.

A hyperlink can be used (amongst other things) to:

- Move to another Web page in the current site
- Move to a new Web site
- Invite e-mail

Hyperlinks are also discussed in the previous section, **Creating Web Pages by Writing HTML Code**. However, in this section, which is based on the use of HTML Editor software such as Microsoft FrontPage, the task of creating hyperlinks is very much simpler.

The files for the three pages to be linked together in the Sailing Club example, **index.htm**, **joining.htm** and **activities.htm** are shown below in their folder:

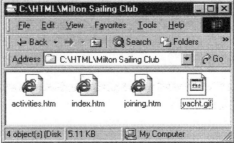

Creating a Hyperlink

We will assume the three pages have already been created and only need connecting with hyperlinks. First the Home Page **index.htm** is loaded into the HTML editor - Microsoft FrontPage Express, etc.

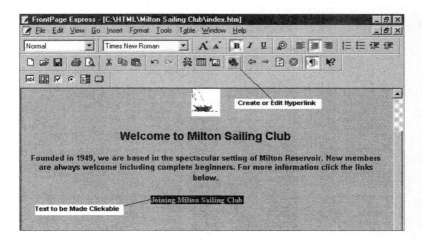

Then you highlight the text to be made "clickable" as shown above. Now click on the icon to create or edit a hyperlink, as shown above and right.

The **Create Hyperlink** feature opens, with 3 tabs at the top, **Open Pages**, **World Wide Web** and **New Page**. The first tab lists the titles of any other Web pages currently open in FrontPage Express. These titles are obtained automatically from the top line of each Web page. If you want to link the current page (in which the hyperlink is being created) to any of these pages, click the title of the open page and then click **OK**.

Links to Web Pages in the Same Folder

If you select the **World Wide Web** tab you can create hyperlinks to many different destinations. The simplest link is to another Web page saved in the same folder as the currently selected Web page (i.e. the page in which you are creating the hyperlink). In this case you just type the name of the page in the **URL:** slot.

Linking to Web Sites On Other Computers

There are many other types of link available and these are revealed when you click the down arrow to the right of **Hyperlink Type:**.

The most commonly used **Hyperlink Type:** is **http:** or **Hypertext Transfer Protocol**. You must include the full URL, for example:

http://www.jimsite.com/milton/news.htm

Apart from **http://** Web sites there are several other possible destinations for links. These include **ftp** (File Transfer Protocol) sites from where it's possible to download files from extensive libraries. Links which encourage a visitor to send an e-mail are discussed shortly.

After any new hyperlinks have been inserted, the page must be saved. Then the page should be loaded into your Web browser (Internet Explorer or Netscape Navigator, etc.), and the links tested.

Inviting E-mails Using mailto:

To encourage visitors to your site to send you an e-mail, a hyperlink can be created which makes this very easy.

- Type a suitable prompt on the screen, such as **Send us an e-mail**. Highlight this prompt. The prompt will be the "clickable" text.

- Click the icon to **Create or Edit Hyperlink** (shown on the right).

- Select the **World Wide Web** tab and choose **mailto:** as the **Hyperlink Type:**.

- Enter the e-mail address to which replies are to be sent, next to **mailto:** in the **URL:** slot.

Create Hyperlink	☒
Open Pages	World Wide Web	New Page
Hyperlink Type:	mailto: ▼
URL:	mailto:jimgatenby@msn.com

- Save the Web page including the new e-mail link.

- Load the Web page into your Internet browser and check that the e-mail link works.

When you click on the link, the installed e-mail program should start up with your e-mail address already infilled ready for a response to be sent.

Creating a Link to a New Web Page

Suppose you have already created a Home Page and now wish to create (and link to) a new page. FrontPage Express makes this simple by including a **New Page** tab in the Create Hyperlink dialogue box. First, working in the Home Page, type in the text which is to be clicked to bring up the new page. In this example, I entered the words **Club** **History**. Highlight this clickable text and then click the **Create or Edit Hyperlink** icon shown left. Select the **New Page** tab, as shown below.

Create Hyperlink	✕

| Open Pages | World Wide Web | New Page |

Page Title: Club History

Page URL: club.htm

Target Frame:

In the above **Create Hyperlink** dialogue box, you can see that FrontPage Express has automatically filled in the **Page Title:** using the words from the clickable text, i.e. **Club History**. It has also decided that the file name for the page, or **Page URL:**, should be **club.htm**. If you don't wish to use the names provided automatically you can type in your own. (**Target Frame:** in the above dialogue box is used when the destination of a link is a specific part of a Web page, i.e. a frame.) After you click **OK** and select **Normal Page**, a new page opens ready for you to enter the content.

When the new page is complete it should be saved. The text **Club History** entered on the Home Page will now be a "live" hyperlink. When you click <u>Club History</u> the new page should be loaded.

Links Back to the Home Page

After you have entered all of your Web pages, you will probably wish to create additional links, as previously described, between pairs of pages. Especially necessary are links to return the visitor from each of the pages to the Home Page, **index.htm**.

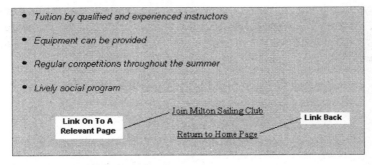

Making an Image into a Hyperlink

An image inserted in a Web page can be made to act as a hyperlink. This graphical link might be used in addition to a piece of clickable text, both screen objects linking to the same destination Web page, etc. Or the image may be a thumbnail or miniature version of a picture. In this case the destination of the link would be a full size version of the picture. As discussed elsewhere, the purpose of the thumbnail is to save waiting for the full size image to load. The latter can be viewed, by anyone interested, simply by clicking the thumbnail.

To use an image as a hyperlink, select the image and click the **Create or Edit Hyperlink** icon shown on the left. The **Create Hyperlink** dialogue box appears from where it is possible to select the destination of the link as described previously.

Save the Web page, including the new graphic hyperlink. Load it into your Web browser. When you move the cursor over the graphic, a hand should appear, indicating that the graphic is a link. Check that clicking the graphic link brings up the required Web page or file.

Creating a Thumbnail Image

A thumbnail image is a special sort of link, in which a very small image, (which loads quickly), can be clicked to view a full size version. Microsoft FrontPage has a built-in feature for creating thumbnail links automatically, as follows:

Load the full size image into the Web page in Microsoft FrontPage.

 Select, i.e. highlight, the image - it will then be surrounded by 8 small squares. The Drawing Toolbar appears, including the **Auto Thumbnail** icon shown on the left and below.

When you click the **Auto Thumbnail** icon, the full size image is reduced to the size of the thumbnail. Then when you save the Web page, you also save both the thumbnail and the full size image, by default in the folder **My Documents/My Webs** or in a folder of your choice. If, for example, the full size image were called **desk.gif**, say, then the thumbnail will be automatically saved with the name **desk_small.gif**. When you open the Web page in your browser, (Internet Explorer, Netscape Navigator, etc.), the thumbnail is displayed.

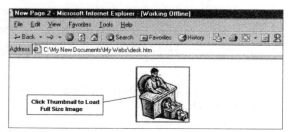

Clicking on the thumbnail brings up the full size image. Click **Back** to return to the Web page containing the thumbnail.

Exercise 7: Entering and Formatting Text and Images and Creating Hyperlinks

1. Start up your HTML editor program with a new Web page open.

2. Enter the following text:

Membership Details

Joining Milton Sailing Club

If you would like more information on joining Milton Sailing Club, please contact the Membership Secretary, as detailed below. Discounts are available for students, pensioners and those on low incomes.

Stella Austin, Secretary
Milton Sailing Club,
Milton M16 6SC Tel. 01273 7249516

Send an e-mail now by clicking on the address below:
stella@milton.co.uk

For a range of new and secondhand equipment click the link below:
View Equipment

Back to Milton Sailing Club Home Page

This Web site is maintained by:

3. Enter your name after: **This Web site is maintained by:**

    Format the text **Membership Details** as a Heading in the large font size.

    Format the text **Joining Milton Sailing Club** as a Subheading in the medium font size.

    Format all of the other text as Body Text in the small font size.

    Ensure that each of the 8 paragraphs is separated by a clear linespace.

4. Format the paragraphs starting **If you would like...**, **Send an e-mail...**, **For a range of ...** and **This Web site is maintained by:** to be left aligned on the page. Format all other paragraphs to be centre-aligned on the page.

    Embolden the text **Send an e-mail now by clicking on the address below:**.

    Italicise the text **new and secondhand equipment**.

5. Import the graphic **yacht.gif** and position it below the text **Membership Details** and above the text **Joining Milton Sailing Club**. Ensure that the graphic is centre-aligned on the page. Adjust the size of the graphic if necessary.

6. Save the new page with the name **joining.htm**.

7. Load the new page into the Web browser and check the appearance and spelling.

8. Return to the HTML editor and correct any mistakes. Change the background and text colours.

9. Save the amended **joining.htm** page to disc.

10. The new page should link back to the **Milton Sailing Club** Home Page. Edit the new page to link the text **Back to Milton Sailing Club Home Page** to the **index.htm** page.

    Edit the text **stella@milton.co.uk** to be an e-mail link.

    Edit the text **View Equipment** to be a link to the web site:

    www.chandlers.com

    Save the amended **joining.htm** page to disc.

11. The Home Page needs to link to the new page. Load the home Page **index.htm** into your HTML editor. In the **index.htm** page link the text **Joining Milton Sailing Club** to the newly-created page, **joining.htm**.

12. Save the amended **index.htm** page to disc.

13. Load the pages **index.htm** and **joining.htm** into your browser (Internet Explorer, Netscape Navigator, etc.) and check that the links between the two pages work.

14. The text for the third Web page, **activities.htm** is shown below. Start a new page in your HTML editor and enter the text.

Club Activities

We can offer:

Tuition by qualified and experienced instructors
Preparation for examinations
Regular competitions throughout the summer
Equipment can be provided
Lively social program

Return to Milton Sailing Club Home Page

Join Milton Sailing Club

This Web site is maintained by:

---

15. Format the page in the same style as the previous two pages, **index.htm** and **joining.htm**, including the three font sizes and suitable text alignment - left, right or centred.

    Use emboldened and italicised text where appropriate.

    Import the **yacht.gif** graphic and align as before.

16. Edit the new page to link the text **Return to Milton Sailing Club Home Page** to the **index.htm** page.

    Edit the text **Join Milton Sailing Club** to be a link to the **joining.htm** page.

17. Save the new page **activities.htm** to disc.

18. The Home Page needs to link to the new page. Load the Home Page **index.htm** into your HTML editor. In the **index.htm** page, link the text **Club Activities** to the **activities.htm** page.

19. Save the amended **index.htm** page to disc.

20. Load the pages **index.htm**, **joining.htm** and **activities.htm** into your browser (Internet Explorer, Netscape Navigator, etc.) and check that the links between all three pages work. (You do not need to test the e-mail and http:// links.)

21. From your browser, print a copy of each of the three Web pages **index.htm**, **joining.htm** and **activities.htm**.

   Print a copy of the HTML code for each of the three pages.

Publishing Your Web Site

At this stage you should have a separate folder containing all of the Web pages and the graphics file necessary for the simple Web site created in the previous exercises. The next stage is to upload the files

to the server of the Internet Service Provider who will host your site. Precise instructions for this task are provided by individual ISPs but the subject is covered in more detail in the final chapter of this book, **Publishing Your Web Site**.

We have now covered the basic skills needed for creating Web pages using an HTML editor. The previous chapter described the creation of Web pages by writing your own HTML code. As both methods cover the same basic skills, the same self-assessment checklist is repeated at the end of each chapter, for convenience.

Most people will prefer the ease of use of an HTML editor for most of their work while occasionally fine tuning the HTML code by hand, in a text editor like Notepad. Word processors can be used to produce HTML code, but they lack the features and versatility of an HTML editor.

Checklist of Basic Internet Skills

This list follows closely the Assessment Objectives of Element 3: Publish Information on a Web Site, of the Internet Technologies Stage 1 course from Oxford Cambridge and RSA Examinations. You might wish to check your progress against this list and, if necessary, revisit any topics requiring further work.

Objective	Achieved
Insert an image into a document, align and resize.	☐
Use 3 different font sizes, small, medium, large.	☐
Embolden specified text.	☐
Italicise specified text.	☐
Align page items as specified - left, right, centre.	☐
Change the background colour of a document.	☐
Link existing pages via specified text.	☐
Link new page to existing pages via specified text.	☐
Link existing pages to new page via specified text.	☐
Link specified text to a specified e-mail address.	☐
Link specified text to a specified URL (http://)	☐
Store the Web pages to disc.	☐
Print Web pages from the browser software.	☐
Print HTML source code for all Web pages.	☐
Exit the software using the correct procedure.	☐

Publishing Your Web Site

Introduction

This is the final phase in the creation of your own Web site. Publishing involves storing your Web site on an Internet server computer which can be accessed by thousands or even millions of people.

By now you should have:

1. Created your Web pages either by writing your own HTML code or by using an HTML editor/Web design program or perhaps a word processor that creates HTML code.

2. Checked the layout, appearance and spelling in the main Internet browsers, namely Internet Explorer and Netscape Navigator.

3. Made any necessary modifications using your text editor or your HTML editor, before resaving the amended files.

4. Tested all of the hyperlinks to other pages and Web sites and to **mailto:** links to e-mail addresses.

5. Saved all of the **.html** files in a new folder, dedicated to the Web site, as shown below. This folder may also contain **.gif** or **.jpeg** graphics files and any other files to be imported into the Web pages.

There are several stages involved in publishing your Web site:

1.   You need to choose a *Web host*. This is a company providing storage space on its Internet *server* computers, to which people can *upload* and save their Web pages. The server computers are accessible to the millions of people who surf the Internet.

2.   So that other people can find your Web pages, you need to obtain and register a *domain name*, which will be used in the unique address or URL (Uniform Resource Locator) for your Web site, such as:

www.jimgatenby.com

3.   You may need to obtain some special software to handle the uploading of your files to the Internet server. This is known as an *FTP client*, File Transfer Protocol being a well-established system for copying files across the Internet.

4.   In order to maximize the number of visitors to your Web site, the site should be registered with the main search engines. You can add keywords and descriptions to your Web pages, increasing the likelihood of your site being found and displayed prominently, near the top of the listings of the results of searches.

The above stages of publishing a Web site are discussed in more detail on the following pages.

Choosing a Web Host

Your Internet Service Provider (the company supplying your normal Internet connection) may well offer some space for storing your Web pages, typically 10-20MB. Some companies offer this service free, although your site may be used for advertising purposes. If you are a private individual and just want to store a few a pages of news and information for friends and relatives, this may be adequate. AOL allows every member to have 2MB of disc space on its servers, giving a maximum of 10 or 14MB per Internet account. (AOL accounts can have up to 7 screen names i.e. users).

If your needs are more demanding, for example because yours is a company Web site, perhaps used for e-commerce, then you should consider the specialist Web hosting companies. There are hundreds of these but to ensure a good service it's probably safest to choose a web host which has been personally recommended or favourably reviewed in the press. Normally there is a startup fee of perhaps £25, including your own domain name. Thereafter there may be a regular monthly fee, depending on your requirements. A small user might pay £12 per month for 35MB of disc space with 10 e-mail addresses. A larger company might need 600MB of disc space with 150 e-mail addresses at a cost of £120 a month.

Apart from the cost of the service and storage available, some other considerations when choosing a Web host are:

- Do they set up your domain name and register it for you?
- Are the Internet servers fast and reliable?
- Is their technical support both accessible and helpful?
- Is their system compatible with all of the features built into your Web pages?
- Can they provide you with the number of visitors to your site?

The following Web sites provide details of Web hosts:

www.tophosts.com   **www.findahost.com,**

www.easyspace.com   **www.freewebspace.net**

Obtaining a Domain Name

The domain name is used in the unique address (URL or Uniform Resource Locator) of your Web site. One type of domain name is based on the Web host's address, such as:

www.webhost.com/jimgatenby

However, a neater solution is to use a *virtual domain*, created by the Web host company, which would be simply:

www.jimgatenby.co.uk/

First, however, you must find out if your chosen domain name has already been taken by someone else. This can be checked by connecting to:

www.networksolutions.com/

The above site can also be used to register domain names, for which there is a registration fee payable. For **co.uk** domain names you can use:

www.nominet.org.uk/

The last part of the domain name consists of the *domain type*, followed by the *country code*, as follows:

Examples of Domain Types

ac	Academic	gov	Government
com	Commercial organization	mil	Military
co	UK commercial organization	net	Internet Service
edu	Universities	org	Non-profit organisation

Examples of Country Codes

au	Australia	jp	Japan
ca	Canada	nl	Netherlands
de	Germany	no	Norway
fr	France	uk	United Kingdom

Putting Your Web Pages onto the Internet - FTP

So your Web site has been created and the files are sitting on the hard disc inside of your own computer in your home, office or college, etc. The files must now be copied across the Internet and saved on the hard disc of a server computer provided by your Web hosting company. The precise destination on the server will be given to you by the host.

Although it is possible to *download* files across the Internet using an Internet browser such as Internet Explorer or Netscape Navigator, *uploading* files requires special software which uses the **File Transfer Protocol** (**FTP**). As its name implies, FTP has been the standard method of moving files around the Internet for a long time. FTP servers around the world contain thousands of files which can be downloaded to your computer. Instead of opening an account with the provider of the FTP site, users are given restricted access to the server using the login name "Anonymous". It's normal to use a person's e-mail address as their password. Then you can browse the directories of files and download any you require, to your computer.

In order to upload your Web site files to an Internet server computer you need a program on your computer to manage the process. This is known as an *FTP client*.

There are lots of FTP client programs, some of which can be downloaded free from the Internet or on a time-limited free trial. Amongst the most popular FTP programs are **CuteFTP (http://www.cuteftp.com/)** and **WS_FTP (http://www.ipswitch.com/)**.

Some HTML editors i.e. Web design programs, have the FTP software already built in. For example, if you select **File** and **Publish** while using Microsoft FrontPage, you are presented with the **Publish Web** dialogue box shown below.

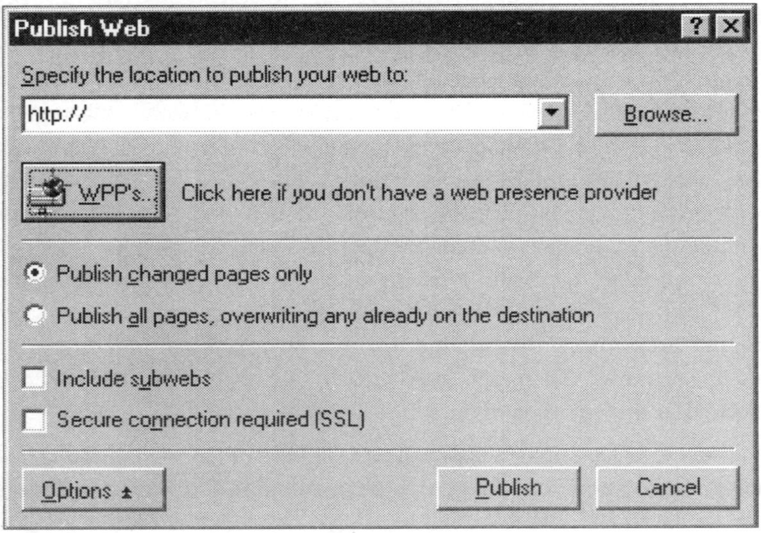

Please note in the above dialogue box that the destination for your Web pages must be specified in the slot after **http://**. If you haven't already chosen a Web host, click the button labelled **WPPs....** This connects your computer to the Internet and displays a list of registered **Web Presence Providers for Microsoft Front Page**, allowing you to choose your Web host. These companies should provide a service which is fully compatible with Microsoft FrontPage and all of its Web page features.

Also notice in the previous dialogue box that in addition to publishing all of the pages for a Web site, you can instead publish only the pages that have changed. This enables a Web site to be updated quickly.

Publishing Web Pages on AOL

AOL makes 2MB of free Web space, called **My Space**, available to each "screenname" or member. Since an AOL account can have up to 7 screennames, this makes up to 14MB available on every AOL account. The procedure for uploading Web pages to this free Web space has been made very simple by AOL. The user is shielded from many of the technicalities involved in using FTP client programs, like logging on with an "anonymous" name. However, AOL also provides the option to download an FTP client program. Then, if you wish, you can do the file transfer work yourself by the traditional FTP method. Both methods of uploading Web pages to an Internet server are discussed in the following pages, using AOL as the Web host.

Uploading Web Pages Using AOL's Own FTP Tool

AOL members first log on to AOL in the usual way. Then **FTP** is entered as a **Keyword**. This opens the **File Transfer Protocol (FTP)** window, shown below.

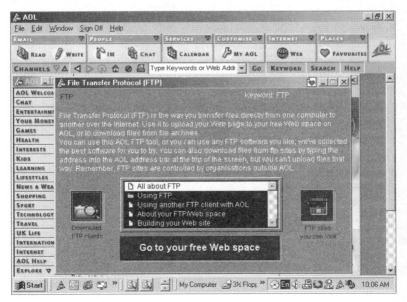

The **File Transfer Protocol (FTP)** window shown on the previous page includes a lot of background information about FTP, for the newcomer to the subject. There is a button to download FTP client programs as an alternative to AOL's own FTP tool.

However, in the context of uploading our own Web pages, we need to select **Go to your free Web space** shown at the bottom of the previous **File Transfer Protocol (FTP)** window. This leads to the user's Web space, which is located at **http://members.aol.com/screenname/**, where **screenname** is the AOL user name or login name.

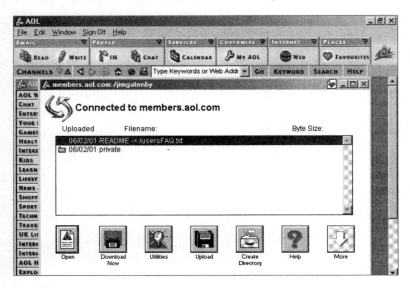

Later the above window will list all of the files for the Web pages uploaded to our Web site. Note also the **Utilities** button, which allows you to delete or rename Web pages from the site and also the **Create Directory** button.

Now click the **Upload** button to start the process of transferring files from your computer to the hard disc on the server computer of your Web host.

A window opens in which you enter, in the **Remote Filename** slot, the name of the first file in your Web site, **index.html** in this example.

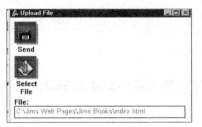

The **Transfer Mode** must also be set. **.html** and other text files are set as **ASCII** while graphics and programs files are set as **Binary**. Click **Continue** and the **Upload File** dialogue box appears, from which you click **Select File**.

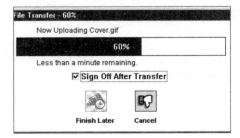

This allows you to select the required file from your own hard disc. The full path to the file is automatically entered at the bottom of the **Upload File** dialogue box shown above. In this example the path is:

C:\Jims Web Pages\Jims Books\index.html

Now click **Send** and the file is copied to your Web space. HTML files are transferred very quickly, but as shown below, bulky graphics files take a lot longer to upload.

The process just described must be repeated for each of the files to be uploaded. At the end of the process your Web space should give details of the uploaded files. Connect to AOL and enter **FTP** as a **Keyword** then **Go to your free Web space**. Your uploaded files should be listed as shown below:

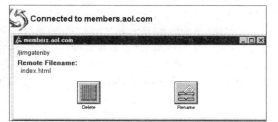

The files I uploaded were **index.html**, **booklist.html** and **cover.gif**. You are now ready to test your Web pages on-line by logging on to the Internet and typing the address: **http://members.aol.com/ pagename.html** into AOL or a Web browser such as Internet Explorer or Netscape Navigator. Any problems will need to be corrected by reverting to the HTML editor or text editor on your own computer. Then you will need to save the corrected file and upload it to your Web space, replacing the previous version on the Web.

Deleting and Renaming Web Pages and Files

The **Utilities** button in the **members.aol.com** window shown previously allows you to delete any Web pages or files you no longer need. You can also **Rename** files and there is a **Create Directory** button.

Using an FTP Program to Upload Your Web Pages

If you wish to control the entire file transfer process yourself, then you need an FTP client program installed on your computer. For subscribers to AOL there's a button for downloading FTP client programs on the main **File Transfer Protocol (FTP)** window shown below on the left.

Otherwise you need to connect to the Web site of the company providing the software. For example, the popular FTP client **WS_FTP** is available from:

http://www.ipswitch.com

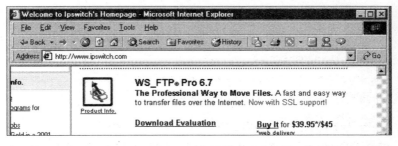

As shown above, there are the usual options to buy the software on-line or to download a free trial version. The trial version expires after 30 days, at which point you can purchase a full version, for a small fee. The downloaded file is placed in your download folder with the name **f_x86t32.exe**. Double clicking its name or icon installs the software on your computer. You can choose to place the icon for **WS_FTP Pro** (shown right) either on the **Windows Desktop** or in **My Computer**.

Once you have installed an FTP client program on your computer, it can be used for file transfer tasks in general, not just the uploading of Web pages currently under discussion.

A typical procedure for using an FTP program is as follows:

- Log on to your Internet Service Provider in the normal way.

- Open your FTP client program and click **Connect**.

- Log on again (while still logged on to your Internet Service Provider), with the user name **Anonymous**, with your **e-mail address** as the password.

- Enter the name of the server which is to host your Web pages.

- Select the files for your Web site from your local hard disc, usually in the left-hand panel of the FTP client.

- Give the command to transfer the files from your local hard disc to the Web host's server. The transferred files appear in the right-hand panel of the FTP client program.

Setting Up WS_FTP

In this example the FTP client **WS_FTP** is used, with AOL as the Web space host. First some setting up of the software is needed. You can select **New Site** (**File** and **New Site...**) and give the site a name and you must enter the **Host Name**.

WS_FTP can be used for file transfers in general, not just Web pages in the .htm or .html format. To ensure that these files are transferred in the required ASCII format used for text files, we need to add **.htm** and **.html** in the **Extensions** tab accessed from **Options** in WS_FTP.

In the main **Connection** window in **WS_FTP** you must enter the **Host Name:** i.e. the Internet server which is the destination for your Web pages. In line with FTP practice, the **UserID:** is **Anonymous** and the password is your e-mail address. The password should be saved.

The setting up process just described is a one-off process, not required in future uploads to your Web site, which will therefore be much simpler.

Copying Files From Your Hard Disc to the Internet Server

The previous setting-up work can be carried out off-line. Next we must log on to our Internet Service provider in the usual way, i.e. with the User Name and Password which are used for normal Internet access.

Now start **WS_FTP** from **Start** and **Programs** and click **Connect**. This will log you onto your Web space, using **Anonymous** as your user name and your e-mail address as the password, saved earlier.

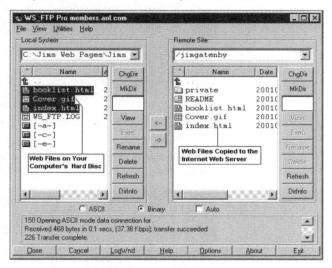

Next browse, in the left-hand panel above, to select from your own hard disc, the files to be uploaded. The **Remote Site** slot shows the destination for your Web pages, on the Internet server. When you click the right-pointing arrow (shown in the middle of the window above), the files are uploaded to your Web space and listed in the right-hand panel above.

Editing a Web site

You can **Delete** or **Rename** Web pages, after highlighting their files in the right-hand panel shown above. The **Rename** and **Delete** buttons are greyed out but just visible. To update Web pages, simply amend the pages on your local hard disc and upload them as previously described.

Attracting Visitors to Your Web Site

A Web site may be created for a variety of purposes. You may wish to share information with friends, relatives or people sharing a common interest or hobby. Alternatively, you might need to publish the results of academic research to as wide an audience as possible. Or your purpose may be purely commercial, with a product or service to sell. Whatever the purpose of your site, you need to encourage as many people as possible to visit.

Once your site is up and running, visitors are likely to arrive from various sources:

- People who type your URL (e.g. http://www.mywebsite.co.uk/) into a Web browser, such as Internet Explorer or Netscape Navigator.

- Surfers who finish up at your Web site after clicking a link on another Web site.

- People who have entered key words into a *search engine* such as Google, or after clicking **Search** in their Web browser like Internet Explorer or Netscape Navigator.

Publicising Your Web Address (URL)

If people are to visit your site after typing your URL in the address bar of their browser, you must publicise the URL as widely as possible. This can be included as a standard addition (or "signature") to all of your e-mails. In the case of a company, the URL should be carried on all of your business cards, stationery and advertisements.

Links From Other Web Sites

Web sites which cover subjects relevant to your own site may find it mutually profitable (in terms of attracting visitors) if your sites are linked in both directions. So, for example, if your site is about the Russian Blue (a breed of cat), contact similar Web sites to arrange links. This should increase the number of visitors to all of the linked sites and also increase the amount of information available to the Web surfer.

Finding Your Site as a Result of a Search

When someone types a key word relating to your site into a search tool such as Excite, AltaVista, or Google, the result of the search may be a list containing hundreds, thousands or even hundreds of thousands of Web pages containing your key words. Obviously if your Web page is well down the list of results, even the most persistent of people will probably give up before looking at your site. (Most of us, apparently, only look at a relatively small number of entries at the front of the list before abandoning a particular search).

Much time and effort has been spent in devising ways of ensuring that a Web page is found by search tools and then placed high in the listing of results. Some of the strategies intended to help your Web site to be promoted in the list of search results are as follows:

- Register your site with the well-known search engines.

- Include in your Web pages relevant and concise key words. These should be in the title and near the top of the page and also scattered frequently throughout the pages.

- Arrange for your site to be linked to other similar Web sites. A site which is the destination of many links will be highly rated and promoted towards the top of search lists.

Search Tools

There are two categories of search tool, namely *directories* and *search engines*. Yahoo and LookSmart are examples of directories, while AltaVista, Lycos, Excite, HotBot and Google are well-known search engines. A search engine contains an index with the contents of millions of Web pages. The search feature in Internet Explorer allows you to use a single search service or a whole battery of search tools.

```
Customize Search Settings
  ⊙ Use the Search Assistant for smart searching
  ○ Use one search service for all searches

  ☑ Find a Web page
  ┌─────────────┐   ☑ MSN Search   ☐ Excite
  │ MSN Search  │   ☑ GoTo.com     ☐ Yahoo!
  │ AltaVista   │   ☑ AltaVista    ☐ Euroseek
  │ GoTo.com    │   ☑ Lycos        ☐ Northern Light
  │ Lycos       │
  └─────────────┘
```

Directories

To register your Web site with a directory, you send them a *description* of your site together with the URL for your site. This is reviewed by an editor who decides whether or not to include the *description* of your site in the directory. When you initiate a search using a directory, only the descriptions are searched to find matches with your criteria. If you subsequently tweak your Web pages (as discussed shortly) in an attempt to improve their prominence in search results, this will make no difference when using a directory. If a search fails using a directory such as Yahoo, you can use a search engine via links at the bottom of the search page. In a directory the results of a search are organized into categories as shown below, when "gardening" was entered into Yahoo.

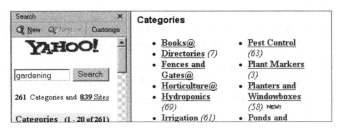

Search Engines

It is usually recommended that you submit the URL of your Web site to all of the major search engines and you will normally have to complete a form containing all of your personal and/or business details.

Search engines use a *crawler* or *spider* to follow every link and visit every page on your Web site. The URLs are added to the search engine index, together with the text from every page visited. The crawler repeats the visits, perhaps every few weeks, to make sure the index is up-to-date. Some people create a *crawler page* for their Web site, which is a listing of all of the URLs to be included in the search engine index. Searching involves looking for key words in every page in the index.

Improving Your Web Site's Ranking in Search Results

There are several ways to get your Web page high up in the lists of search results. These include using short and relevant key words or phrases near the top of each page, especially in the **<title>** and **<meta>** tags. For example, to promote a Web site on garden design:

<title>garden design</title>

<meta name="description"content="garden design">

<meta name="keywords"content="garden design">

The text in the title tag normally appears in the first line of your site's entry in a search results list, as the link to your Web site. The text in the meta description usually appears in the results list just below the link. These words must capture the interest of a person when they scan the results list after a search. If the words don't seem relevant, concise and meaningful, the person searching the Web will probably not bother to visit your site.

You should also allow for likely spelling mistakes. For example, all sorts of attempts are made at my seemingly straightforward name, from Gatesby to Gattonby to Gately. So likely spellings and misspellings of any key words should be included in the **<title>** and **<meta>** tags.

You can also scatter key words generously around the Web pages. However, If this is overdone it is regarded as cheating or "spamming" and may cause your pages to be ejected by the search engine staff.

Appendix

The Internet Technologies Stage 1 Course

The following syllabus has been reproduced with the permission of Oxford Cambridge and RSA Examinations. The syllabus consists of the following three Elements and associated Assessment Objectives:

Use Electronic Mail For Business Communication

1.1 Transmit messages electronically: reply, forward, multiple send, copy, attach file, use address books, save and print.

1.2 Receive messages electronically: access and store message and attachment, store address, delete message.

1.3 Use appropriate software accurately: select appropriate software, enter data, access mail server, print messages and attachment.

Use the Internet for On-Line Research

2.1 Navigate the World Wide Web to access remote data: navigate using hyperlinks, access specific pages, store and retrieve address.

2.2 Use on-line search techniques to retrieve remote data: use local and general search engines, retrieve specified data, retrieve specified page.

2.3 Use appropriate software accurately, select appropriate software, print Web pages.

Publish Information on a Web Site

3.1 Compose and edit a Web page: create Web page, insert image, use emphasis, align page items, change background colour.

3.2 Create a Web Structure: link pages, add new page, add external link, add e-mail link, test links, store Web pages.

3.3 Use appropriate software accurately: select appropriate software, enter data, print source code, print Web pages.

More information about the Information Technology Stage 1 course is given on the next page.

Obtaining Further Information

Many students take Internet Technologies Stage 1 at a Further Education or Business College. Some schools also offer such courses, often as Adult Education Classes in the evening or for a few hours in the day time. Further details of Internet Technologies Stage 1 and many other IT courses (such as the popular CLAIT computer literacy course) can be obtained from:

> OCR (Oxford Cambridge and RSA Examinations)
>
> Westwood Way
>
> Coventry
>
> CV4 8JQ
>
> www.ocr.org.uk

Publications

The OCR Web site listed above has a full list of publications available to the general public and there is an on-line order form. The relevant publications for Internet Technologies Stage 1 are:

N474   Internet Technologies Stage 1 '00 Information Brief

L204   Internet Technologies Stage 1 '00 Tutor's Handbook and Syllabus

G021   Internet Technologies Stage 1 '00 Sample Assignments

Index